Help Yourself

How to take advantage of your learning styles

Gail Murphy Sonbuchner

NEW READERS PRESS
Publishing Division of Laubach Literacy International
Syracuse, New York

Note: Gender specific pronouns are rarely used in this book. When they are used, however, male and female pronouns appear in alternating chapters.

ISBN 0-88336-555-3

New Readers Press
Publishing Division of
Laubach Literacy International
Box 131, Syracuse, NY 13210

Printed in the United States of America

Project Editor: Christina M. Jagger
Manuscript Editor: Elizabeth Costello
Publication Assistant: Jeanna H. Walsh
Book design and illustrations: Patricia Rapple
Cover design: Steve Rhodes
9 8 7 6 5 4 3 2

Acknowledgments

To Hugo F. Sonbuchner, an invaluable ally, for his specialized guidance and creative additions.

To Christina M. Jagger, Senior Editor of Reading and Writing at New Readers Press, for her superb editorial guidance and her extensive knowledge of the learning process.

Table of Contents

To the Reader

I desire that there be as many different persons in the world as possible; I would have each one be very careful to find out and preserve his own way.

HENRY DAVID THOREAU

Celebrate your individuality! You have your own combination of learning strengths and weaknesses. *Help Yourself* will help you to discover your personal learning strengths and introduce you to a variety of strategies to take advantage of them.

Strategies are the "how you think" and "what you do" to get things done. As you discover more and more strategies that work for you, you will develop flexibility in using them. As you become more skilled at using them, you will be able to combine them in new ways; you will develop the adaptability needed to succeed in our ever-changing world.

Have fun with this book as you learn to *Help Yourself!*

Gail Murphy Sonbuchner

Gail Murphy Sonbuchner

Eight Steps to Using This Handbook

Step 1. **Read Chapter 1** and take the learning styles inventory. You'll discover your preferred learning styles and how to take advantage of them.

Step 2. **Read Chapter 2** for suggestions on creating the best work environment for *you*.

Step 3. **Ask yourself, "What am I having trouble with?"**

Example: "I can't remember what I've studied when I get to the test."

Step 4. **Turn to the Table of Contents**. Find the chapter that deals with your problem area.

Example: Test Taking

Step 5. **Look for a question that deals with your problem area.**

Example: Question E: "What can I do when I blank out during a test?"

Step 6. **Turn to the page number listed by that question.**

If you haven't chosen a question, but you know the general area of the problem (test taking), turn to the first page of that chapter and:

A. Complete the checklist.

B. Choose the checked statement that is the most important to you and note the letter to the right of your check mark. Turn to the section in the chapter that begins with that letter.

Step 7. **Select a strategy to try.**

A. Choose a strategy that features one of your preferred learning styles in the left-hand column.

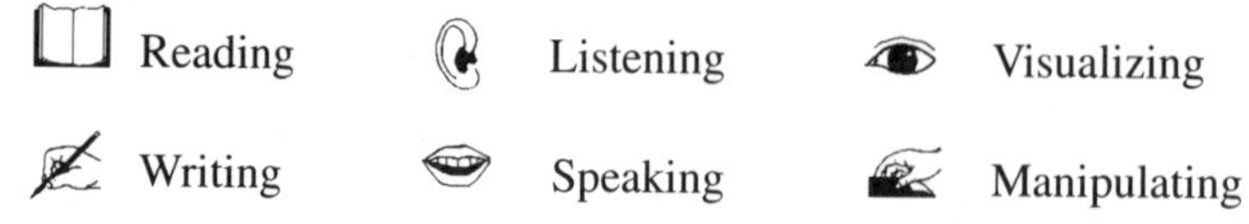

B. Follow the directions in the center column that explain the strategy.

C. Look at the right-hand column to get more information and additional hints about that strategy.

Step 8. Try the strategy you have chosen four or five times to see if it works for you. If it works but you need more help, try another strategy to use with it. If it doesn't work for you, cross out the number of that strategy so you don't use it again. Select another strategy and give it a try. *Help Yourself!*

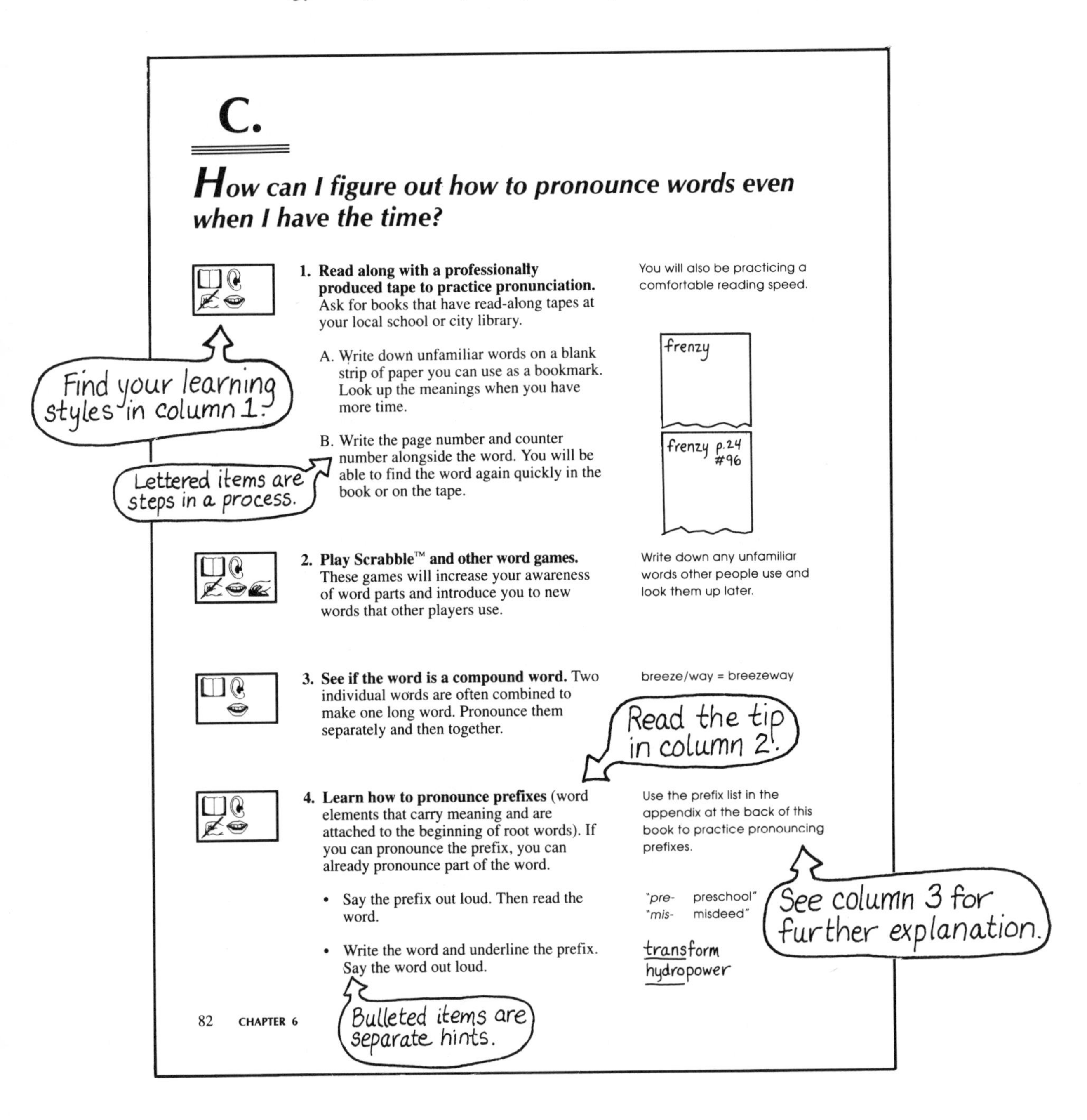

C.

How can I figure out how to pronounce words even when I have the time?

1. **Read along with a professionally produced tape to practice pronunciation.** Ask for books that have read-along tapes at your local school or city library.

   You will also be practicing a comfortable reading speed.

   A. Write down unfamiliar words on a blank strip of paper you can use as a bookmark. Look up the meanings when you have more time.

   frenzy

   B. Write the page number and counter number alongside the word. You will be able to find the word again quickly in the book or on the tape.

   frenzy p.24 #96

2. **Play Scrabble™ and other word games.** These games will increase your awareness of word parts and introduce you to new words that other players use.

   Write down any unfamiliar words other people use and look them up later.

3. **See if the word is a compound word.** Two individual words are often combined to make one long word. Pronounce them separately and then together.

   breeze/way = breezeway

4. **Learn how to pronounce prefixes** (word elements that carry meaning and are attached to the beginning of root words). If you can pronounce the prefix, you can already pronounce part of the word.

   Use the prefix list in the appendix at the back of this book to practice pronouncing prefixes.

   - Say the prefix out loud. Then read the word.

     "*pre-* preschool"
     "*mis-* misdeed"

   - Write the word and underline the prefix. Say the word out loud.

     transform
     hydropower

82 CHAPTER 6

CHAPTER 1

Finding Your Preferred Learning Styles

What does "learning styles" mean?

Not everyone learns well in the same way. Some learn best by reading. Others learn best by listening. Still others learn best when they watch demonstrations or do projects. "Learning styles" refers to the variety of ways people take in, store, and retrieve information. Your learning styles can give you clues about how to best approach a particular task.

In order to take advantage of your learning styles, you need to determine what they are. The *learning styles inventory* on the next two pages will help you figure out which learning styles you use most often.

Each group of five statements on the next two pages represents a different learning style. Read each statement. If you think the statement describes you, put a check mark (√) on the line to the left. If you think the statement does not describe you, leave the line blank. Don't think about each statement too long; your first response is likely to be the most accurate.

After you have read all the statements and checked the ones that apply to you, count up the number of check marks in each group and write the number in the space provided. The groups that have the most check marks represent your best learning styles. The section called "Interpreting the inventory" (page 16) will show you how to use the results of this inventory and make the most of your learning styles.

Learning Styles Inventory

Group 1

___ 1. I like to read when I have free time.
___ 2. I like to read a report rather than be told what's in it.
___ 3. I understand something best when I read it.
___ 4. I remember what I read better than I remember what I hear.
___ 5. I would rather read a newspaper than watch the news on TV.

_____ **Total number of check marks in Group 1**

Group 2

___ 1. I take notes when I read to better understand the material.
___ 2. I take lecture notes to help me remember the material.
___ 3. I like to recopy my lecture notes as a way of better understanding the material.
___ 4. I make fewer mistakes when I write than when I speak.
___ 5. I find the best way to keep track of my schedule is to write it down.

_____ **Total number of check marks in Group 2**

Group 3

___ 1. I like to listen to people discuss things.
___ 2. I learn more when I watch the news than when I read about it.
___ 3. I usually remember what I hear.
___ 4. I would rather watch a TV show or movie based on a book than read the book itself.
___ 5. I learn better by listening to a lecture than by taking notes from a textbook on the same subject.

_____ **Total number of check marks in Group 3**

Group 4

___ 1. I remember things better when I say them out loud.
___ 2. I talk to myself when I try to solve problems.
___ 3. I communicate better on the telephone than I do in writing.
___ 4. I learn best when I study with other people.
___ 5. I understand material better when I read it out loud.

_____ **Total number of check marks in Group 4**

Group 5

___ 1. I can "see" words in my mind's eye when I need to spell them.
___ 2. I picture what I read.
___ 3. I can remember something by "seeing" it in my mind.
___ 4. I remember what the pages look like in books I've read.
___ 5. I remember people's faces better than I remember their names.

_____ **Total number of check marks in Group 5**

Group 6

___ 1. I like to make models of things.
___ 2. I would rather do experiments than read about them.
___ 3. I learn better by handling objects.
___ 4. I find it hard to sit still when I study.
___ 5. I pace and move around a lot when I'm trying to think through a problem.

_____ **Total number of check marks in Group 6**

Interpreting the inventory

This book deals with six basic learning styles: reading, writing, listening, speaking, visualizing, and manipulating. You probably use a combination of several learning styles as you go about your work. The learning styles inventory is designed to point out your *strongest* learning styles. Look over the inventory you took. In which groups do you have the most check marks?

If you had three or more check marks in Group 1, *reading* is one of your preferred learning styles. You find it easier to learn information by reading printed words.

If you had three or more check marks in Group 2, *writing* is one of your preferred learning styles. You learn information more easily when you express it in written form.

If you had three or more check marks in Group 3, *listening* is one of your preferred learning styles. You find it easy to learn information that you hear.

If you had three or more check marks in Group 4, *speaking* is one of your preferred learning styles. You are best able to learn when you express yourself out loud.

If you had three or more check marks in Group 5, *visualizing* is one of your preferred learning styles. Your mind's eye is a very powerful learning tool for you. You learn well when you use your brain to "photograph" information.

If you had three or more check marks in Group 6, *manipulating* is one of your preferred learning styles. You learn well when you are able to handle objects you're learning about. Manipulating situations by changing your location, moving around, etc., also helps you to learn.

Each of the next six pages focuses on one learning style. Turn to the pages that feature your preferred learning styles to find general suggestions for taking advantage of the ways you learn best. Read about any learning style in which you had three or more check marks. These are your strongest learning styles and you should use them whenever you can.

Reading

If *reading* is one of your preferred learning styles, you take in, store, and retrieve information more easily when you can see it and read it yourself.

As you work with chapters 3 through 10, look for learning tips that have this symbol: 📖

Below are general suggestions for how to take advantage of this style.

- Read a chapter before you listen to the lecture on it.
- Read a book or article about a topic instead of attending a lecture.
- When you watch demonstrations, take good written notes. Later, you can refresh your memory by reading your notes.
- Get information for reports by reading instead of watching videos or listening to speeches.
- Read your notes, study guides, and flash cards over and over again.
- Back up what you hear by taking notes that you can refer to again.
- Read directions instead of having someone tell you how to do something.
- Read information yourself instead of having someone read it to you.
- Look up words you don't know the meaning of in a dictionary instead of asking someone what they mean. You'll be more likely to remember the meanings.
- Make travel plans by reading maps and travel guides.
- Choose a job that requires more reading than listening.

Writing

If *writing* is one of your preferred learning styles, you take in, store, and retrieve information more easily when you write it down.

As you work with chapters 3 through 10, look for learning tips that have this symbol: ✍

Below are general suggestions for how to take advantage of this style.

- "Pencil read" by reading with a pen/pencil in your hand. Underline and take notes as you read. "Talk to yourself" in writing.
- Take good lecture notes.
- Recopy your lecture notes in your own handwriting.
- Choose to do written reports instead of giving speeches whenever possible.
- Write down the steps you need to follow in order to complete a project.
- Keep track of your schedule with a calendar system and write down commitments.
- Write lists of things you need to do.
- Carry a small notebook with you, so you can take notes to remember what you have read or heard.
- Write people letters instead of calling them on the telephone.
- Choose a job that involves more writing than listening or speaking.

Listening

If *listening* is one of your preferred learning styles, you take in, store, and retrieve information more easily when you hear it.

As you work with chapters 3 through 10, look for learning tips that have this symbol:

Below are general suggestions for how to take advantage of this style.

- Never miss a class. Listening to the information you have read about will help you to understand it better.
- Listen to information about a topic on videotape, TV, or an audiotape.
- Tape a lecture, so you can listen to it again.
- Read out loud the information you are studying.
- Interview people about the subject you are studying.
- Have another student read his notes to you.
- Study with other people. Discuss ideas and give each other oral tests.
- Discuss your notes, directions, or manuals out loud with yourself.
- Use a tape recorder to quiz yourself.
- Repeat information out loud after hearing it.
- Have someone read your tests to you or read them out loud to yourself.
- Call people on the telephone instead of writing to them.
- Choose a job in which listening plays an important part.

Speaking

If *speaking* is one of your preferred learning styles, you take in, store, and retrieve information more easily when you talk about it.

As you work with chapters 3 through 10, look for learning tips that have this symbol:

Below are general suggestions for how to take advantage of this style.

- Don't miss classes. You can ask questions about what is said.
- Dictate into a tape recorder what you need to write or study.
- Ask yourself questions out loud while you are studying.
- Study information by saying it out loud and discussing it with yourself.
- Study with other people, so you can discuss the information.
- Study for a quiz by asking questions out loud and answering them.
- Choose to give a speech rather than do a written report whenever possible.
- Repeat things right after you hear them to help you remember them.
- Calm your nerves by saying positive things to yourself.
- Call people on the telephone instead of writing to them.
- If you are having trouble spelling a word, spell it out loud before you write it.
- Choose a job that requires speaking rather than writing.

Visualizing

If *visualizing* is one of your preferred learning styles, you take in, store, and retrieve information more easily if you can picture something in your mind's eye.

As you work with chapters 3 through 10, look for learning tips that have this symbol: 👁

Below are general suggestions for how to take advantage of this style.

- Close your eyes and practice "seeing" what you need to remember.
- Watch movies or videos on a subject, so you will have an easier time "seeing" the information again.
- As you read something, picture how it would look if you were seeing it in a movie.
- Watch demonstrations of things you need to do instead of reading about them, so you will be able to visualize them later.
- As you study diagrams and maps, close your eyes and "see" them again.
- Take special note of the shape of things you want to remember.
- Solve simple math problems by visualizing the numerals.
- Close your eyes and "see" a word you need to spell before you write it.
- Calm your nerves by picturing yourself calm and in control in that particular situation.
- Remember telephone numbers by studying them until you can "see" them in your mind's eye.
- Visualize your tasks on the job to more clearly understand what you need to do.

Manipulating

If *manipulating* is one of your preferred learning styles, you take in, store, and retrieve information more easily if you can handle things and/or change your environment.

As you work with chapters 3 through 10, look for learning tips that have this symbol: ✍

Below are general suggestions for how to take advantage of this style.

- Build models of hard-to-understand concepts.
- Experiment by doing things you read about.
- Watch someone do what you need to learn before trying it.
- Type a research paper on a typewriter or computer.
- Watch demonstrations instead of reading or hearing about them.
- Visit a place you are learning about.
- Given a choice, build a project rather than write a report about it.
- Do math problems with an abacus or with objects you can move.
- Make sure your work area allows you to move around while you study.
- Be flexible with your time schedule, so you can change plans and expectations when you need to.
- Choose a job that allows you to work with your hands and to move around.

Which learning style is best?

No one learning style is better than another. The key to using learning styles wisely is to be aware of which you prefer and which will work best for you in a particular situation. Read below to see how seven different people use a variety of learning styles.

Sharon doesn't like to read, so she chooses the *listening* and *speaking* styles of learning.

Eric always chooses to *write* a report instead of giving a speech because he is self-conscious about making errors in front of people. As his speaking skills improve, he may switch to *speaking*.

Jason has a job in the middle of a busy, noisy shopping mall. His job requires that he use *listening* and *speaking,* his weaker methods. He backs them up with *reading* and *writing,* his preferred methods, by carrying a notebook with him and writing down what he needs to remember. When he needs to discuss something, he moves to a quieter location *(manipulating)*.

Brenda has a hard time getting down on paper what she wants to say. Since she is a good speaker, she pretends she is giving a speech and dictates it into a tape recorder *(speaking)*. She writes down what she has said *(writing)* as she listens to the tape playing back *(listening)*.

Mike learns easily by *reading*. His instructor shows a movie *(listening)* and tells him that there will be a test on it. He backs up his listening by taking good notes *(writing),* so he can review what he has learned by reading his notes *(reading)*.

Charles is a basketball player. He actively uses many learning styles during a game. He *listens* to the coach and studies diagrams of the plays *(reading)*. He talks with his teammates *(listening* and *speaking)* while playing the game *(manipulating)*. When Charles is on the bench, he closes his eyes and "sees" himself taking shots and making baskets *(visualizing)*.

Maria is planning a visit to a new vacation spot several hundred miles from her home. She studies a map to plan her route *(reading)*. She traces the route she will take with a marker (*writing*). She then closes her eyes to "see" her map *(visualizing)*. Before she starts out, she telephones ahead to check on reservations (*listening* and *speaking*). While on the road, she encounters a detour and stops at a filling station to inquire about how to get back on the right route (*listening*, *speaking*, *manipulating*). All six learning styles play a part in helping Maria to reach her goal.

Your key to success is to decide how you are going to *take in* information and how you are going to *express* yourself. Don't classify yourself as being able to use only one learning style. You want to be able to use a variety of styles, depending on the particular task and the surroundings you need to work in. If you are not succeeding with the style you are using, you need to switch to another learning style. *Think flexibility!*

CHAPTER 2

You and Your Work Environment

When you have work to do, where do you do it? At the kitchen table? On the couch? In a quiet corner somewhere? When you're working, do you need total quiet, or do you like a little noise? Do the surroundings in which you usually work allow you to do your *best* work?

Whether you need to tackle a school assignment such as writing a paper or a household task such as paying bills, it's important to work in the right environment. Since people respond to the conditions around them in different ways, it helps to take the time to design the work environment that is best for you. This process involves finding the harmony between your personal characteristics and your surroundings.

This chapter will help you pinpoint your best working conditions and will give you suggestions for creating those conditions. When you're working in the right environment, you'll find that your efficiency, effectiveness, and comfort level increase.

The statements on the next page will help you determine your best work environment. Some ask you to consider your personal traits; others ask you to consider the conditions you prefer.

Read each pair of statements. Put a check mark on the line to the left of the statement in each pair you most agree with. Then look on pages 27 through 36. Find the statement you checked and read the hints for designing your work environment.

Motivation

__ 1. It's easy for me to get motivated to do my work.
__ 2. It's hard for me to get motivated to do my work.

Concentration

__ 1. It's easy for me to concentrate.
__ 2. It's hard for me to concentrate.

Length of study sessions

__ 1. I like to do my work in long sessions of two hours or more.
__ 2. I like to do my work in short sessions of no more than 45 minutes.

Involvement with others

__ 1. I learn best when I study alone.
__ 2. I learn best when I study with others.

Level of organization

__ 1. I like my work area to be messy. I know where everything is.
__ 2. I like my work area to be very organized. Messiness bothers me.

Prime times

__ 1. I do my best work in the daytime.
__ 2. I do my best work at night.

Amount of noise

__ 1. I like to have some noise in the background while I work.
__ 2. I need absolute quiet while I work.

Amount of light

__ 1. I like to work in a brightly lit area.
__ 2. I like to work in a dimly lit area.

Amount of heat

__ 1. I like to work in a warm room.
__ 2. I like to work in a cool room.

Food and drink

__ 1. I work best when I have food and/or something to drink handy.
__ 2. I don't need food and drink while I work.

Motivation

It's easy for me to get motivated to do my work.

If you checked this statement, you have a big advantage. Many people find that the most difficult thing about getting their work done is getting started on it. If you don't have a problem with becoming motivated, just keep doing what you've been doing.

It's hard for me to get motivated to do my work.

If you checked this statement, you're not alone. Many people have a hard time getting started, especially when faced with a task that's difficult or unpleasant. It can be hard to "get going."

If you have a hard time getting motivated, try these suggestions. Set goals for what you need to accomplish in each work session and write down a detailed time schedule. Then, when you achieve one of your goals, give yourself a reward. For example, after putting in a two-hour study session, reward yourself by watching your favorite half-hour TV show.

Concentration

It's easy for me to concentrate.

If you checked this statement, you're one of the few people who can concentrate in any place, at any time. You can tune out everything around you. You aren't distracted by what is going on around you in the same room.

If you are this type of person, you have the luxury of being able to study in comfortable chairs, on couches, in noisy rooms, or in any place where you are comfortable.

It's hard for me to concentrate.

If you checked this statement, you need to be very careful in choosing your work environment. You need to eliminate all possible distractions.

Keep your work area clear of everything except what you need to do your work. Work away from people and noise. This will put you in a "this is business" frame of mind. Clear away anything that might draw your attention from the task at hand: magazines, favorite photographs of family and friends, a radio, etc.

Length of study sessions

I like to do my work in long sessions of two hours or more.

If you checked this statement, you can work for long periods of time without losing your concentration. You may sit down to work and two hours later wonder how it got so late. Time flies by!

If you are able to work for long periods of time, you should organize everything in your work area. Put a "do not disturb" sign on the door to your work area, turn the volume down on the telephone, and lose yourself in your work. Be careful, though, that you don't get so caught up in your work that you forget other responsibilities. Set an alarm clock if you'll need to stop work at a certain time.

I like to do my work in short sessions of no more than 45 minutes.

If you checked this statement, you need to vary your work sessions.

Schedule short breaks in between school assignments and household chores. Work on a job that requires you to sit still for awhile. Take a ten-minute break. Then switch to a task that requires some movement, such as vacuuming or exercising. Take another ten-minute break before returning to your studies. Make sure you go back to the books, though. The key to your success is returning to work after each of your short breaks.

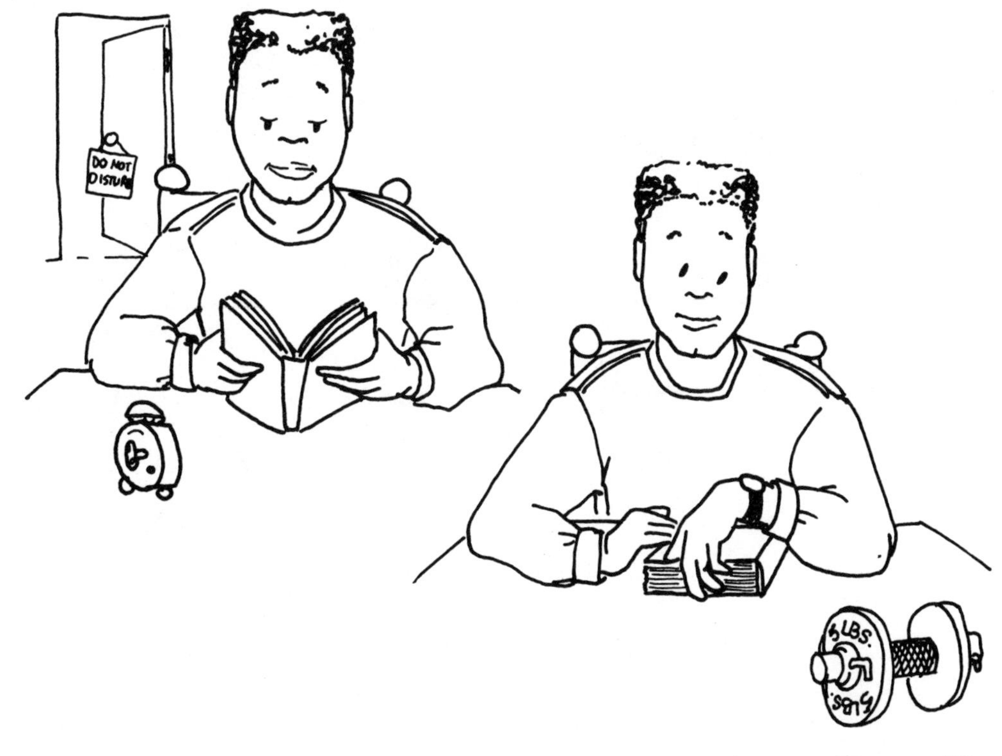

Involvement with others

I learn best when I study alone.

If you checked this statement, you are probably someone who is very confident about what you need to study and how you need to study it. Reading, writing, and visualizing are probably your preferred learning styles. Studying with other people will only confuse you.

If you learn best when you study by yourself, by all means do so. But be sure to include group activities in other areas of your life.

I learn best when I study with others.

If you checked this statement, you need the company of others to keep you focused on your studying. You're probably someone who learns best by listening and speaking. You remember more of what you study when you discuss it with other people.

If you're the type of person who likes to study with others, put together a study group. Work on group projects whenever you can. If you happen to be working alone and you get stuck, call someone to discuss what you're doing.

Level of organization

I like my work area to be messy. I know where everything is.

If you checked this statement, it doesn't mean that you're a messy person. It just means that you like to have everything right out in front of you rather than tucked neatly away in drawers or on shelves. You probably like to work in what's often called "organized disorganization." Your work area may *look* messy to others, but you know where everything is and are comfortable with it.

Make sure, though, that your work area is off-limits to others. They may be tempted to clean it up, which will only make you feel uncomfortable and unable to work. The best thing to do is work in a room that can be closed off. That way, your messiness won't bother anyone and others won't bother you.

I like my work area to be very organized. Messiness bothers me.

If you checked this statement, you work best in a highly organized area. A messy room tends to make you feel nervous, unsettled, and unable to work. Find a room or corner to work in and keep it free of clutter. When you've finished a study session, put all your materials back in their proper place. That way, you won't need to spend time cleaning up the next time you sit down to work.

Prime times

I do my best work in the daytime.

If you checked this statement, you're a day person. You are more alert and able to organize your thoughts during the daylight hours. As soon as it gets dark, your energy level goes down. Things are harder to remember, new ideas come more slowly, reading takes longer, and it's harder to get interested in studying.

If you are a day person, schedule work and study time during the daylight hours whenever possible. This may mean getting up early in the morning to do your studying instead of staying up late at night. Schedule your most difficult jobs during the morning. Save your leisure activities and easier work for the evening hours.

I do my best work at night.

If you checked this statement, you're a night person. You probably have a hard time getting up in the morning and don't get a lot of work done early in the day. Afternoon is a more efficient time for you, and the evening hours are your most productive.

If you are a night person, schedule your most difficult and demanding jobs during the evening hours. Do your studying at night rather than getting up early to study. Tackle chores that require less concentration during the day.

Amount of noise

I like to have some noise in the background while I work.

If you checked this statement, quiet rooms probably make you nervous. You will most likely enter a room and immediately turn on the radio or TV, so it's not quiet. Noise helps you get your work done faster.

If a noisy environment is for you, you will want to work in rooms with a TV on or music playing. When you need supreme concentration, however, for tasks such as memorizing, check your environment carefully. If you can name the song playing on the radio or follow the conversation going on around you, the noise level is interfering with your work.

I need absolute quiet while I work.

If you checked this statement, you need to get rid of any noise in your environment in order to concentrate and do your best work. Make an effort to find a quiet area whenever you need to get down to business. If you find yourself in a noisy environment, wear earphones or earplugs. Work away from people, TVs, radios, and a lot of activity. Create a quiet area where you can "shut out the world" and get your work done. Try going to a library. If you are given study time in a noisy classroom, ask for permission to go somewhere else to work.

Amount of light

I like to work in a brightly lit area.

If you checked this statement, you are more alert in bright light, whether it's sunlight outside or artificial light inside. As soon as the sun goes down, your energy level decreases.

If you are a person who needs bright light, sit near a window, have a bright light in your room, or have a bright light shining down on you and your work. Work in a room with light-colored walls. Remove heavy curtains from the windows if they block out a lot of light. When you need to calm down and relax, go into an area that is dimly lit.

I like to work in a dimly lit area.

If you checked this statement, bright light probably makes you feel jumpy. You are more comfortable in dim light, so you're more productive. You need to be careful, however, to avoid eyestrain by having adequate light for the work you are doing.

If you are a person who prefers dim light, sit away from windows, have your reading light shine on your work and not on you, and put dimmers on your light switches. If you have a choice, work in rooms that have darker walls. Select curtains that block out bright light, but not all of the light. Adjust window shades or blinds to control the amount of light. If you are in a room with fluorescent lights, turn on only half of them. Sit in the area that has the dim light.

Amount of heat

I like to work in a warm room.

If you checked this statement, a cold area probably causes you to lose concentration. You are likely to end up focusing on keeping warm, instead of on your work.

If you operate more efficiently in a warm room, wear sweaters or long underwear whenever it's cool. If you work in both warm and cool rooms, layer your clothing so you can bundle up or take some clothes off. Keep the heat turned up or plug in an electric heater that you can direct toward your work area. Try to work in rooms that are decorated with warm colors like red and orange. These colors make a room seem warmer.

I like to work in a cool room.

If you checked this statement, warm areas probably make you feel sleepy and unmotivated. Cool areas make you want to work and allow you to think more clearly.

If you thrive in cool areas, work in a cooler room whenever you have a choice. Wear layers of clothing, so you can remove some whenever the temperature gets too warm for you. Pull shades down against the sun and open windows when it's cool outside. Try to work in a room decorated with cool colors like blue and green. These colors make a room seem cooler.

Food and drink

I work best when I have food and/or something to drink handy.

If you checked this statement, you probably find yourself interrupting your work to get up and find something to snack on. Snacking while you work is fine, but try to gather your snacks *before* you start your study session. This will keep you from taking up too much time on your "snack breaks."

I don't need food and drink while I work.

If you checked this statement, you probably don't interrupt your studying with trips to the kitchen for something to eat or drink. When you reach a convenient stopping point in your work session, however, you might want to consider having a healthy snack. Your brain needs food for energy. After a snack, you'll return to your studies refreshed.

CHAPTER 3

Organization and Time Management

What work do you need to do? When do you need to have it done? How can you get it done?

Some people can organize many things and manage much of their time without even thinking about what they are doing. They get up at a specific time, catch the bus, spend a day at work, and meet a friend for a game of basketball. This requires the organization of time, transportation, and supplies! Parents, in particular, are often masters of organization. They juggle the schedules of household members, meals, family appointments, their jobs, and social commitments.

For other people, organizing everything they need to do can seem overwhelming. They need to put a lot of thought into how to approach their many commitments. They need to create systems for keeping track of schoolwork, bills, and other responsibilities.

Do you need tips for getting organized? Fill out the checklist below. Sit back and think about each statement. Be honest! This is your personal survey, so it can only help you if you are honest about yourself.

Put a check mark in front of the statements that describe you:

____ A. It is difficult for me to keep track of all my commitments.

____ B. I have trouble making good use of my time.

____ C. I don't get enough work done during the time I study.

____ D. I don't know what to do with all my papers and study tools.

____ E. I don't have a budgeting system for paying bills.

____ F. My classwork and notes are disorganized.

____ G. I tend to waste time doing normal, everyday tasks.

Choose the checked statement that is the most important to you at this time and note the letter to the right of your check mark. Turn to the section of this chapter that begins with that letter. Look for strategies that have the symbols for your preferred learning styles pictured in the left-hand column. Choose one of these strategies and follow the directions in the center column. Read the comments in the right-hand column for more hints. Try the strategy four or five times to see if it works for you. If it doesn't, try another. Strategies can be used individually or in combinations. Help yourself!

A.

How can I keep track of everything I need to do?

Calendars are a good way to keep track of your schedule. There are calendars that hang on the wall, with plenty of room to write in under each date. There are also small calendars you can carry with you. You don't need expensive calendars, but choose ones that will work best for you.

1. **Set up a household calendar** if you need to keep track of your family.

   A. Keep this large calendar in a central location.

   Make it convenient for everyone to write on.

   B. Have members of your household fill in their own activities and where they'll be.

   You can reach them quickly and/or make plans.

   C. Plan a meeting time for all household members to discuss the next week's calendar (transportation, activities).

   Write down any special needs that affect others in the household.

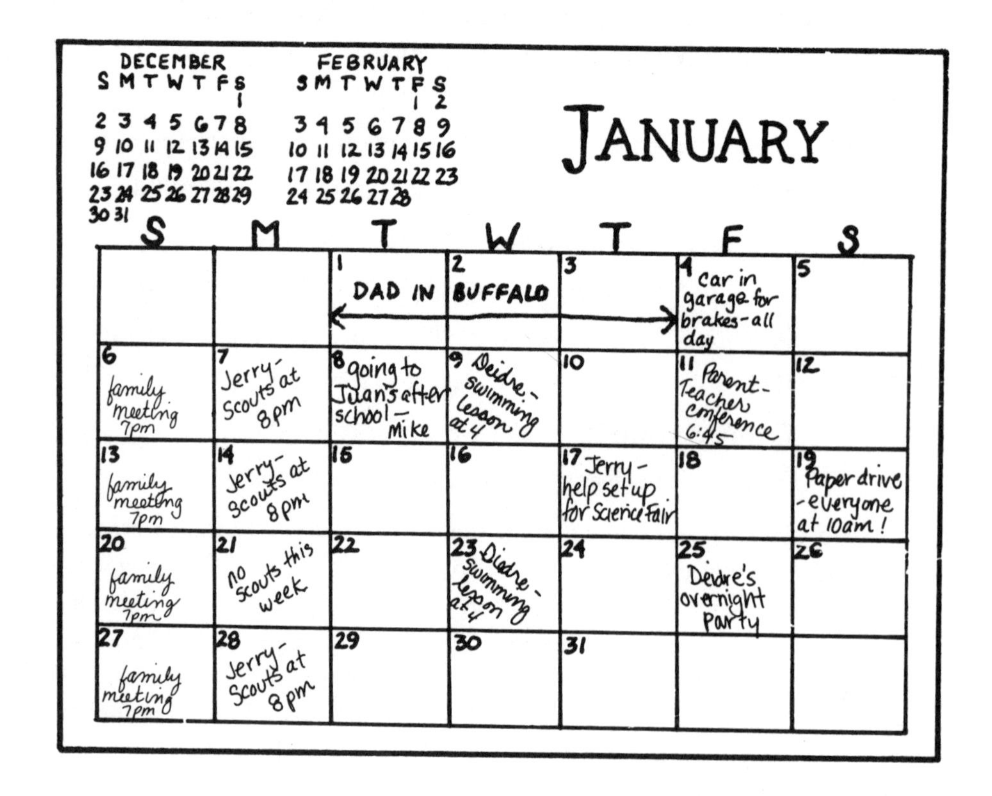

2. **Set up a personal calendar** to keep track of your own activities.

   A. Keep this large calendar in your work area.

   Write down only the things that involve you.

   B. Start with dates you're sure of:

   - Paydays

     Write down the amount.

   - Household bills due dates

     Gas, rent, phone, electricity

   - Charge account due dates

     Mail payments one week before they are due, so they arrive in time.

   - Birthdays/other special days

     Mail cards or gifts one week in advance.

   C. Keep track of activities and classwork.

   - Activities

     Appointments, entertainment

   - Classwork

     Tests, projects, due dates

DECEMBER

S	M	T	W	T	F	S
						1
2	3	4	5	6	7	8
9	10	11	12	13	14	15
16	17	18	19	20	21	22
23	24	25	26	27	28	29
30	31					

FEBRUARY

S	M	T	W	T	F	S
					1	2
3	4	5	6	7	8	9
10	11	12	13	14	15	16
17	18	19	20	21	22	23
24	25	26	27	28		

JANUARY

S	M	T	W	T	F	S
		1 rent due	2	3	4 payday	5
6	7 Scout meeting 8pm	8	9 Math mid-term	10	11 conference at school 6:45pm	12 party at Rashid's 7:30 pm
13	14 pick up Sean at 2pm Scouts at 8pm	15 gas and electric bills due	16 Dr. White 4pm	17 Marla's birthday	18 payday	19
20	21 - no Scouts -	22 car payment due	23 mail card to mom + Dad	24	25 book report due	26
27	28 Mom + Dad's Anniversary #32	29	30	31		

3. Set up a small pocket calendar.

A. Carry it in your pocket, purse, car, briefcase, or backpack.

Keep it where you will see it often.

B. Write in things from the household calendar that you need to do away from home.

- Pick up Sean: 2 PM
- Dr. White: 4 PM

C. Write in things from your personal calendar that you need to remember.

Marla's birthday: 17th

D. Each night, put a small self-stick paper in the front of your pocket calendar. On it, list things you must do the next day.

List things you didn't get done today.

B.

How can I make better use of my time?

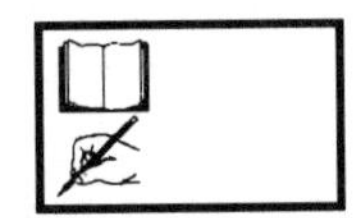

1. **Fill out a time log each week** with things from your personal calendar to find out how you are actually using your time.

Look at the log on the next page as an example.

- Educational commitments

Classes, tests, due dates

- Other commitments

Appointments, work, meetings, recreation

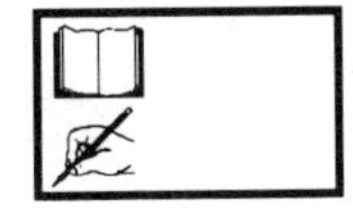

2. **Keep adding and changing things** during the week.

   A. Block out time to prepare for your commitments.

   - Tests: study time

   "2 hrs. for history test"

   - Birthday party: shopping time

   "Party is Tuesday, so I'll need to shop by Monday."

   B. Outline the empty squares so you'll be able to see free time easily.

   C. Adjust your schedule as new events come up.

   "Rod's party is Tuesday night, so I'll get up early and type my paper."

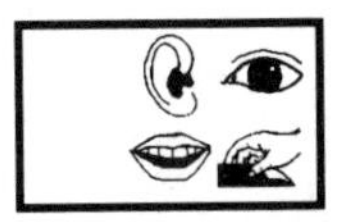

3. **Take advantage of your learning style.**

- If you learn best by listening and speaking, it helps to go over your schedule out loud.
- If you learn best by visualizing, "take a picture" of your schedule. You'll be able to see your calendar in your mind's eye.
- If you learn best by manipulating, it helps to cross out items as you complete them.

Time Log

	Sunday	Monday	Tuesday	Wednesday	Thursday	Friday	Saturday
Early morning							
8:00 am			type paper				
8:30 am				study			
9:00 am							
9:30 am		call dentist					work on book report - due next Thursday
10:00 am							
10:30 am	church	school	school	school	school	school	
11:00 am							
11:30 am							
12 NOON		lunch w/ Brenda					
12:30 pm						school field trip	meet Juan, Deidre + Gina at Mall
1:00 pm		study for history test					
1:30 pm							
2:00 pm							
2:30 pm							
3:00 pm	study						
3:30 pm		shop for Rod's party		work			
4:00 pm							
4:30 pm							
5:00 pm							
5:30 pm	go to Mom + Dad's for dinner	work	work		work	work	
6:00 pm							
6:30 pm							
7:00 pm							
7:30 pm							
8:00 pm					meeting w/ Mr. Straub		
8:30 pm		study	Rod's party	~~game~~ reschedule for Friday (make phone calls)		game	
9:00 pm							
9:30 pm					study		
10:00 pm							
10:30 pm							
Late evening							

C.

How can I get more done during my study time?

Many people waste study time because they don't take enough control of their environment. They don't manipulate their situations to make study time more efficient. All the strategies below involve the learning style "manipulating." Even if manipulating isn't one of your preferred learning styles, give some of the tips below a try. They may show you ways to help yourself.

1. **Study during your alert times.** Decide what time of day you get the most done.

   Do laundry and other activities when you are less alert.

   - Alert in the morning?
     Get up early to study and read.

     You're a "morning person."

   - Alert in the evening?
     Study after dinner.

     You're a "night person."

2. **Always study in the same place.** Your mind will be ready to study as soon as you sit down in that place.

   Don't study in bed; you may fall asleep instead of studying, or you may not go to sleep easily later on.

3. **Clear your study area.** Put away anything that might cause your mind to wander.

   - Magazines
   - Bills
   - Mail

4. **Gather all the materials you will need before you start to study.** Don't waste time looking for them later.

- Paper
- Ruler
- Texts
- Erasers
- Pens
- Dictionary
- Index cards
- Stapler

5. **Start with your hardest subject.** You will have more energy, so it will be easier and get done faster.

If history is hardest for you, get it done right away.

6. **Take study breaks.** Take a break every hour or between subjects. Study breaks improve your concentration.

Be careful not to spend more time on breaks than on your studies!

7. **Figure out what is keeping you from studying.**

Do something about it.

• Bored?	Do something else.	Switch to a different subject.
• Hungry?	Get a snack.	Keep snacks near you.
• Tired?	Exercise.	Get more sleep tonight.
• Need to talk?	Call a friend.	Limit your talk to 10 minutes.

D.

How can I set up my work area?

1. **Purchase a filing cabinet or box and file folders.** Keep them in your work area.

   A. Write headings on the file folders. Be exact in your labeling so you can find things quickly.

   You'll be able to organize papers quickly. You won't lose them or need to guess where they are.

   B. Make sure all the information you'll need is in the folders.

   When filing a bill, for example, date and file it with other relevant papers.

2. **Equip your work area to meet your needs.** The following list has suggestions for any work area.

   How much you need depends on you.

- Pencils/pens
- Pencil sharpener
- Highlight pens
- Tape
- Index cards
- Rubber bands
- Ruler
- Stapler
- Staples
- Paper clips
- Stationery
- Envelopes
- Stamps
- Tape recorder
- Blank cassette tapes
- Calculator
- Dictionary
- Thesaurus
- Typewriter
- Paper: scratch, typing, loose leaf

E.

How can I organize my budget and bills?

1. **Put bills where you can see them.** Leave them in full sight until you pay them.

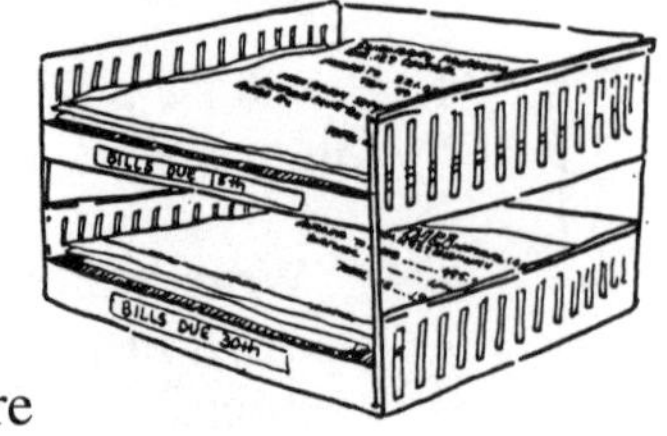

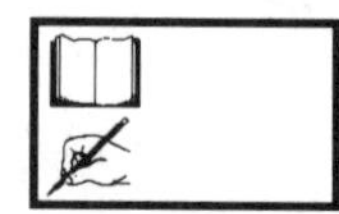

2. **Write notations on each receipt** as you are paying it.
   - Date
   - Amount
   - Check number

12/12/91
$20.00
#5936

3. **Chart your monthly budget.** Make a list like the one at the bottom of this page.

   A. Write down each of your monthly payments.

   B. If you know the amount and due date in advance, fill them in as well. Otherwise, fill in those columns when you receive the bill.

   C. Based on how often you are paid, decide which paycheck each bill needs to be paid out of.

Paycheck of the 15th

Bill	Amt.	Due date
Car payment	$178.00	22nd
Telephone		
Heat		
Savings	$10.00	

Paycheck of the 30th

Bill	Amt.	Due date
Rent	$400.00	1st
Credit card		
Electricity		
Savings	$10.00	

4. Attach all correspondence to the bill it concerns.

- Date every paper when it arrives.

This date may be different from the date on the bill or letter.

- Keep the original.

Make photocopies to mail.

- Keep notes on telephone conversations.

Write down:
- the date
- the name of the person you spoke with
- what was said

General Tip:

Open a savings account. You can save money toward:

- School tuition
- Bills you don't pay every month
- Insurance
- Gifts
- Unexpected expenses

You need to have money set aside for emergencies and other bills. Saving just $10.00 from each paycheck will give you a cushion.

F.

How can I organize my class materials?

1. First day:

A. Buy your books right away.

Bookstores *do* run out.

B. Buy a separate notebook for each class.

Don't mix papers together from different classes.

- Write your name and telephone number in each notebook.

Your notebooks quickly become valuable.

- A three-ring binder makes it possible to reorder the pages and add materials.

You can add:
- Paper
- Returned quizzes, tests
- Handouts from class
- Pocket folders, dividers

- Buy two pocket folders for each class. Label one "Work Done," and the other one "Work Due."

Don't stuff papers in your textbooks. They are easily lost or ruined.

2. During the grading period:

- Do your own marking in your textbook. If it's already highlighted, do yours in a different color.

Read it through before highlighting. That way, you'll know what is important enough to mark.

- Keep track of your grades. Write these on the "Work Done" folder.

It is important to know how you are doing in the class.

- Keep your work organized.

Use your "Work Done" and "Work Due" pocket folders every day.

- Keep adding to your folder.

Add handouts and tests as you get them.

3. After completing the class:

Transfer all of the materials from the class into a pocket folder. Label it, date it, and file it on a shelf or in your filing cabinet or box.

You may want to refer to this material at a later date.

G.

What are some general time-saving tips?

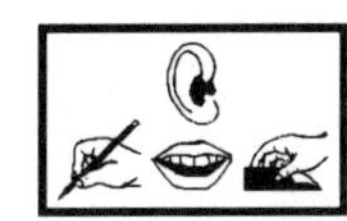

1. Time-saving personal tips:

- Keep your body healthy, so you can move and think quickly.
  - Well-balanced meals
  - Exercise
  - Adequate sleep
- Write notes to yourself on self-stick note papers. Put them where you are sure to see them.

  They come in a variety of sizes and colors.
- Carry a calculator with you.

  They are small, inexpensive, and save time.
- Keep a small notebook with you. Write down things you need to remember.

  Slip one into your purse, briefcase, or glove compartment.
- Call ahead whenever possible.

  Make sure a store has what you need before you make a trip.
- Ask someone for help to save time.
  - Directions
  - What a word means
- Keep a supply of items you know you'll need.

  Buy several birthday cards at once. File them under "cards."

2. Time-saving scheduling tips:

- Pick times you are wide awake to do jobs that need careful work and concentration.

  If you are tired, the job will take longer and won't be done as well.
- Schedule favorite jobs in between jobs you don't like to do. You'll work faster to get to the one you like!

  Change oil in the car in between your favorite yard work and tennis.
- Do two jobs at once when one job requires waiting.
  - Read while doing laundry.
  - Study while waiting for an appointment.

3. Time-saving household tips:

- Store items you seldom use in large, sturdy boxes of the same size, so they stack easily.

  Label them clearly on the end that you will see when they are stored on a shelf.

- Organize your shopping. Put a large self-stick pad by your household calendar. When someone notices an item is running low, he can write it down.

  When one paper fills up, start another one!

- Create a message center. On each message write:

  - Time
  - Message
  - Who the call is for
  - Who took the call

  Write each message on a separate piece of paper or on a self-stick paper the person can see easily and take with her.

CHAPTER 4

Memory

"The professor is so absentminded! She never remembers to close her door or take her hat!" exclaimed the frustrated lab assistant.

"Absentminded?" her friend laughed. "No way! She just doesn't care about shutting doors or remembering her hat. You watch her. She remembers what she *wants* to remember!"

It's easy to remember what you *want* to remember. Sometimes, though, you need to remember things you don't want to, or you may have so much to memorize that you're not sure how to do it. You need memory strategies to train your brain to remember things. You need to develop habits that exercise your memory. The strategies presented in this chapter can help you acquire those habits. With plenty of exercise, your memory will grow stronger.

Read the following statements dealing with the area of memory. Sit back and think about each statement. Be honest! This is your personal survey, so it can only help you if you are honest about yourself.

Put a check mark in front of the statements that describe you:

____ A. I forget the names of people I meet.

____ B. I can't remember the telephone number I just looked up.

____ C. I forget locations and where I put things.

____ D. I need different memory strategies to use when studying.

____ E. Vocabulary, dates, and facts are hard for me to remember.

____ F. I have trouble finding different ways to remember things.

Choose the checked statement that is the most important to you at this time and note the letter to the right of your check mark. Turn to the section of this chapter that begins with that letter. Look for strategies that have the symbols for your preferred learning styles pictured in the left-hand column. Choose one of these strategies and follow the directions in the center column. Read the comments in the right-hand column for more hints. Try the strategy four or five times to see if it works for you. If it doesn't, try another. Strategies can be used individually or in combinations. Help yourself!

How can I remember the names of people I meet?

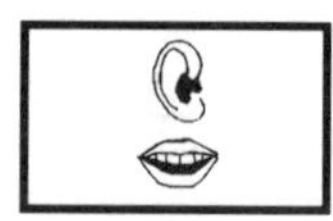

1. **Repeat the person's name out loud** as soon as possible after you have heard it. Think about the name as you repeat it.

"That's an interesting point, Sharon."

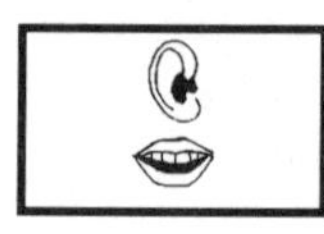

2. **Spell the name to yourself.** Repeat the whole name before and after you have spelled it.

Sharon Hilts
S-H-A-R-O-N H-I-L-T-S
Sharon Hilts

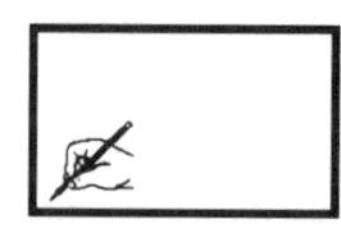

3. **Write the name down somewhere** as soon as possible, then transfer it to a more appropriate place—address book or notebook.

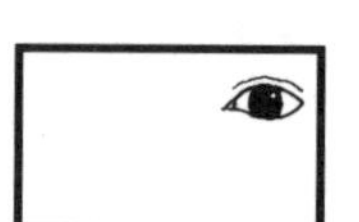

4. **Visualize the person's first name** when you meet her. Looking at her, "see" her name printed above her head. You can always ask what her last name is later.

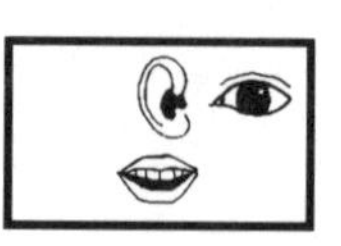

5. **Make up a silly association about it.** The sillier it is, the easier it will be to remember. Repeat the association out loud several times. If visualizing is one of your strengths, create a silly picture. If listening and speaking are your strengths, make the association rhyme.

"Short Sharon Hilts is on stilts!"

B.

How can I remember telephone numbers?

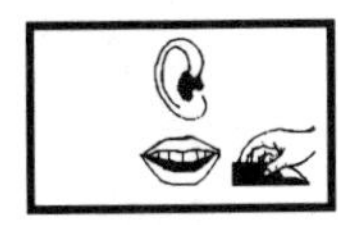

1. **Divide the number into parts.** Say it out loud.

Divide 326-5792 into:
3-2-6
57
92

2. **Say the number out loud five times.** Pause, and repeat it five more times.

Repetition is the key to remembering things.

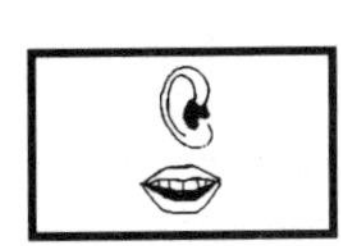

3. **Say the number in a rhythm.** It will sound like a chant at a sporting event.

4. **Keep writing the number.** Write it:

   A. Right after you hear or read it.
   B. Again while it is ringing.
   C. Five more times after you have hung up.

This is an emergency measure! It will focus your thoughts on the telephone number.

5. **Visualize the number.** Close your eyes and "see" the number in your mind's eye.

6. **Practice dialing the number.**

Do this 10 times a day for five days.

   A. Say the party's name out loud.

"Jim"

   B. Say the number out loud as you touch the buttons.

"326-5792"

General Tip: **Quiz yourself throughout the day**. After you feel you know the number, quiz yourself once a week. When you have remembered the number easily for several weeks in a row, quiz yourself once a month.

Memorizing the person's name *and* number together can make it easier: Jim, 326-5792.

C.

How can I remember where I've put things?

General Tip: **Put things in places that make sense to *you!*** Don't follow someone else's organization if it doesn't seem right to you.

Always put things back in the same place.

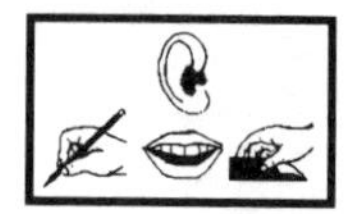

1. **Cue yourself by making associations.**
   Read the following examples to get ideas of how to make up your own cues.

   - Car parked in a huge lot:
     Notice the location in relation to something that cannot be moved. Write it down. Repeat it out loud several times to yourself.

     "My car is straight out from the 'C'."

   - Your seat in a movie theater:
     Count the number of rows from the back of the theater.

     Don't rely on people because they might move!

   - Insurance cards:
     Keep them behind the license in your wallet.

     Keep together things that are associated with each other.

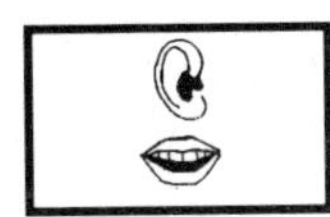

2. **Tell yourself where you are putting something.** This will help you remember where you put it.

"I am putting the stamps in the desk drawer."

3. **Group things that belong together** in one place. It's easier to group things if you think about how a large department store groups things into separate departments.

   - Writing supplies
     - Paper
     - Pencils
     - Notecards
   - Personal care items
     - Deodorant
     - Toothbrushes
   - Credit cards
     - Gas cards
     - Major credit cards
   - Hobby materials
     - Painting supplies
     - Woodworking supplies
   - Holiday items
     - Halloween
     - Thanksgiving

4. **Organize your file folders to fit your individual needs.** Write the appropriate heading on each folder.

   - Taxes
   - Bills
   - Warranties
   - Health insurance
   - Car insurance
   - Car repair receipts
   - A file for each person in the house

File papers in the appropriate file every day.

D.

How can I memorize more successfully?

1. **Use as many of your senses as you can while you are studying.** Create a multi-sensory learning situation by using as many of your learning strengths as possible.

Read it.
Say it out loud.
Write it.
Listen to it.
Visualize it.
Manipulate it.

2. **Choose carefully the subject you'll study next.** Choose one that is not like the one you just finished studying. You don't want to confuse the information.

Don't study chemistry formulas right after you have studied math formulas.

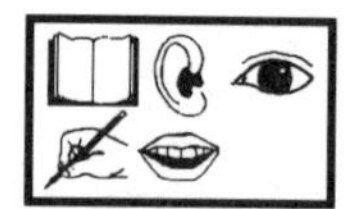

3. **Remember the three Rs:**

READ REPEAT REVIEW

A. Read your notes and study guides carefully. Make sure you can pronounce all of the words and that you know what they mean. If listening is one of your strengths, read your notes out loud. If visualizing is one of your strengths, try to visualize your notes.

Test yourself using the three Rs.

B. Repeatedly read your notes during the day. When you think you know them so well you can't learn any more, study some more. Overlearn the material.

Study your notes in short sessions. Read them and then put them away for a while. Go back and do the same thing again.

C. Review your notes twice a week.

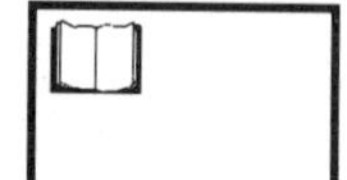

4. **Pay close attention to the author's signals in the book.**
   - Introduction
   - Headings
   - Pictures and captions
   - Summary
   - Numerals/letters
   - Maps/graphs
   - Bold or italicized print

Authors use different types of print, colors, and graphics to point out important information.

5. **Review** by writing everything you can remember about the topic.

Check your notes to see if you have included all important material.

6. **Visualize what you need to memorize.** "Photograph" it in your mind.

   - If it is a diagram or chart, picture it with each label in place.
   - If it is a map, picture its shape and the turns it takes.

General Tip: **If you're having trouble memorizing, ask yourself these questions:**

- How do I feel?

If you're tired, a walk can give you energy. If you're bored, do something different for a while. The strategies may work better when you've had a change of pace.

- What would happen if I didn't memorize this?

You may decide you can get along fine without committing it to memory.

E.

How can I memorize vocabulary, dates, and facts?

Flash cards are a good tool for memorizing small bits of information like vocabulary definitions, dates, and facts. No matter what your learning style, flash cards can help.

1. **Make a set of flash cards.** Use index cards or small sheets of paper.

Flash cards are easy to carry with you and have many uses.

Front:	Back:	Front:	Back:
• Vocabulary	• Definition	scrutinized	looked over carefully
• Event	• Dates	World War I	1914-1918
• Names	• What they did	Nat Turner	led slave rebellion
• Steps or parts	• What they are	parts of plant	root stem leaves seed

(Make a note if you must know them in a certain order.)

2. **Test yourself often.**

   A. Read “Front” out loud.

   B. Give your answer.

   C. Turn the card over to “Back” to check your answer.

- Right answer: go on to next card.
- Wrong answer: keep studying it until you’re right.

3. **Separate the cards into two piles.** As you test yourself, put the cards you answer correctly five times in the “I know” pile. Put cards you answer incorrectly in the “Must study” pile. When all the cards are in the “I know” pile, review the whole pack again.

“I know” pile

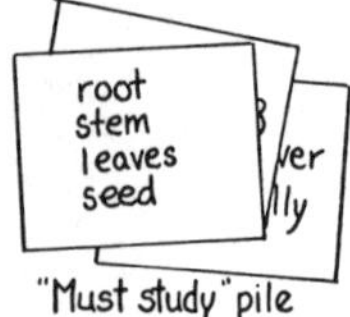

“Must study” pile

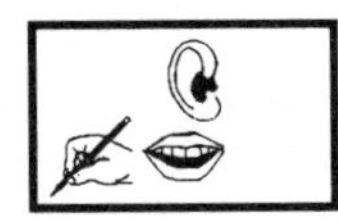

4. **Use the answer in a sentence.** Write the sentence down, or say it out loud. When you can comfortably use the information you are learning, you truly understand it.

"The manager scrutinized our work."

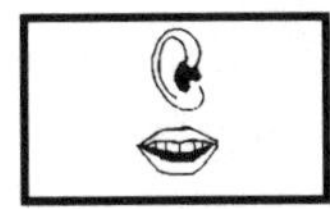

5. **Practice the flash cards with someone else.** One of you can be the teacher while the other one is the student. Then reverse roles.

- Have a contest to see who gets the most right.
- Make up tests for each other.
- Talk about the information.

General Tip: **Reverse the order in which you study the flash cards, so you are prepared to give the answers either way on a test.**

A. Read the question and test yourself on the answer.

B. Read the answer and test yourself on the question.

Practice the flash cards with someone else.

F.

What memory devices can I use?

1. **Create a memory word** to help you memorize a list of items. Use the first letter of each item in your list to create your memory word. Use capital letters so you know it's a memory word. Write the memory word on the front of a flash card. Write what the letters stand for on the back.

HOMES for the names of the five Great Lakes (*Huron, Ontario, Michigan, Erie, Superior*)

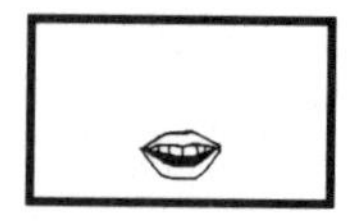

2. **Pronounce the word the way it is spelled,** not the way it is usually pronounced.

Wednesday = "Wĕd/nĕs/dāy"

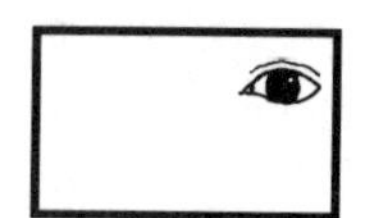

3. **Visualize.** "Photograph" the information in your mind's eye, so you can "see" it again.

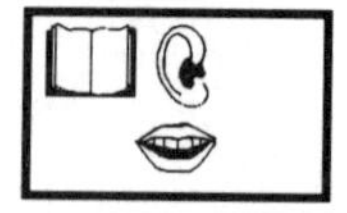

4. **Discover how the words are related.** Repeat the relationship out loud.

Beach and sea
"B*ea*ch and s*ea* each have '*ea*.'"

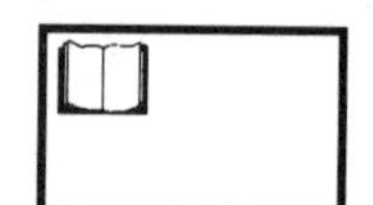

5. **Look for clues in the word that have to do with its meaning.**

H*ear* (with your) *ear*

6. **Repeat the information to a rhythm.**

A good example is the alphabet (ABC) song.

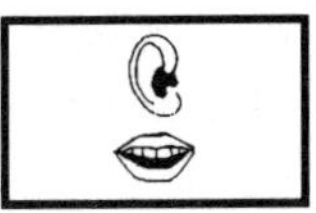

7. Say a "rap" to remember memory strategies.

"I can RAP to remember...

"I can feel it with my TOUCH...

"I can close my eyes and VIS-U-A-LIZE...

"I'll make a mnemonic* using my own jive...

"And repeat it and repeat it 'til it comes alive..."

* A mnemonic (nĭ / mŏn´ / ĭk) is a memory device.

8. **Make up a crazy sentence** using the first letter of each word. The crazier the sentence, the easier it will be to remember.

    - Write the sentence.
    - Visualize the picture it creates.
    - Repeat the sentence out loud.

For the five Great Lakes, a good sentence is, "Make each octopus swim home."

CHAPTER 5

Listening

Hearing is something physical we do without thinking. Listening is a skill we choose to use when we want to remember or make sense out of something we hear. We need to actively involve our minds and focus on what we are hearing to become good listeners.

We use the skill of listening when we share information, plan get-togethers, talk about family matters, set up appointments, or explain to another person how something works. We keep our relationships alive by listening to someone's problem, helping someone with a project, or following directions to someone's house or business. Listening plays an important part in many different areas of our everyday lives. The strategies in this chapter can help improve your vital listening skills.

Read the following statements about the area of listening. Sit back and think about each statement. Be honest! This is your personal survey, so it can only help you if you are honest about yourself.

Put a check mark in front of the statements that describe you:

____ A. I don't know how to use my listening strengths when I study.

____ B. I have trouble understanding directions given to me orally.

____ C. I have a hard time remembering information I hear.

____ D. It's hard for me to concentrate on what a speaker is saying.

____ E. It's difficult for me to understand what a speaker is saying.

____ F. I don't take good lecture notes.

____ G. I don't know how to show people I am listening to them.

____ H. I need ways to improve my listening skills.

Choose the checked statement that is the most important to you at this time and note the letter to the right of your check mark. Turn to the section of this chapter that begins with that letter. Look for strategies that have the symbols for your preferred learning styles pictured in the left-hand column. Choose one of these strategies and follow the directions in the center column. Read the comments in the right-hand column for more hints. Try the strategy four or five times to see if it works for you. If it doesn't, try another. Strategies can be used individually or in combinations. Help yourself!

How should I study if I remember things more easily when I hear them?

1. **Study with someone else.** Discuss information and give each other oral tests.

   Be careful that you don't spend more time socializing than studying!

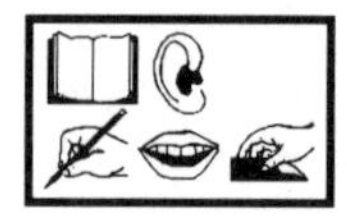

2. **Use a tape recorder to make up self-tests.**

   A. Dictate your questions and answers into the recorder.

   1. Read the question. Count to five silently.

      "When did the Civil War take place?" 1-2-3-4-5

   2. Read the answer. Count to five silently.

      "1861-1865" 1-2-3-4-5

   3. Read another question and answer using the same method.

   B. Test yourself by answering the questions you recorded in writing or out loud.

   1. Listen to the question. Push "pause."
   2. Give the answer. Release the pause button. Listen to the answer and check it against the one you have just given.

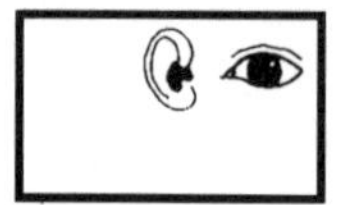

3. **Watch and listen to videos, films, and filmstrips.** Ask your teacher and librarian for suggestions.

   Use these in addition to your regular textbook. Check with your school and city libraries.

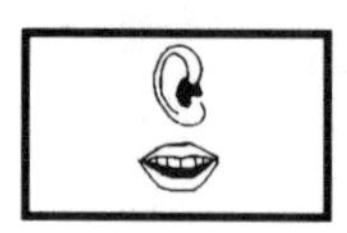

4. **Ask another student to read his class notes to you**. You will be able to ask him questions if you don't understand something.

   You won't have to try to read someone else's handwriting.

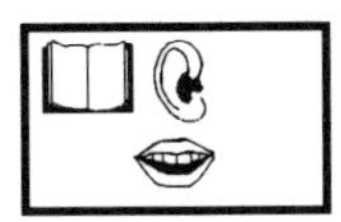

5. **Read the information out loud.** Say it over and over again. Take a break. Then read it out loud again.

Repetition is the key to remembering information. Study it this way three or four times every day.

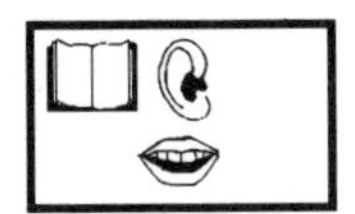

6. **Get tapes of the book you are reading.** Read along as you listen to them. Discuss the information with your family or friends.

Ask your local librarian to help you get the tapes.

Use a tape recorder to make up self-tests.

B.

How can I stop confusing oral directions?

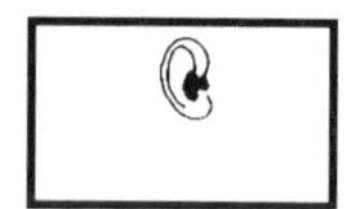

1. **Concentrate on the directions.** Stop any work you are doing. Tell yourself you are going to remember the directions.

"I am going to remember how to get to Carla's house."

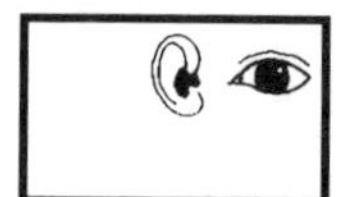

2. **Visualize what you are being told.**

Mentally drive the route to Carla's house as you hear the directions.

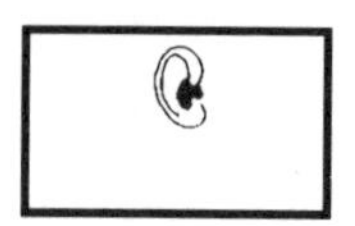

3. **Look at the person who is speaking.** The speaker's facial expressions and gestures will help you understand and remember the directions.

- Is he pointing?
- Is he demonstrating something?
- Is he showing you where to put something?

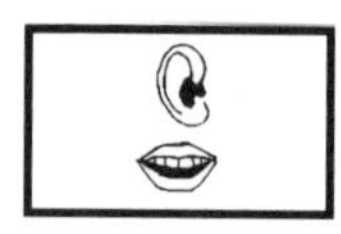

4. **Ask questions.** Ask them as soon as possible whenever you don't understand something.

Don't give yourself a chance to confuse directions.

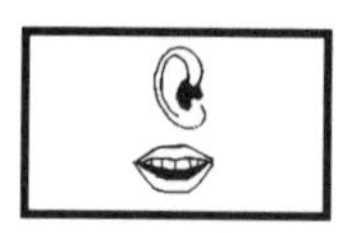

5. **Repeat the directions to yourself.** It helps to put the directions in your own words.

If you have to repeat them, you will pay closer attention to what is said.

6. **Write down words and phrases.** These things are always important to remember when following directions:

This is called "pencil listening!"

- Dates — July 29
- Places — Room 301, Holiday Inn
- Times — 8:30 AM sharp!
- What to bring — Pencil, paper

7. **Carry a pocket notebook with you.** Write down anything you need to remember.

Write down key words and keep repeating them to yourself.

8. **Write directions on your calendar.** You can transfer them to a self-stick paper and take them with you.

July 29
8:30 AM
Holiday Inn
Rte. 494 to Hwy 100 to exit 6.

Repeat the directions to yourself.

C.

What can I do to remember information I hear?

Does information you hear go "in one ear and out the other"? Does it seem to go "over your head"? Remembering information you hear requires effort on your part. You need to do something with the information as soon as possible so it is meaningful to you. It is easier to remember things when they make sense to *you*.

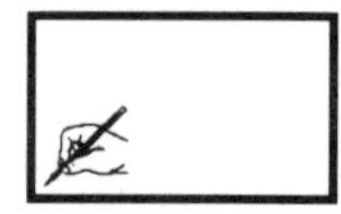

1. **Write a note to yourself on anything handy.** You can write it in a more appropriate place later.
   - Napkin
   - Bank stub
   - Matchbook cover

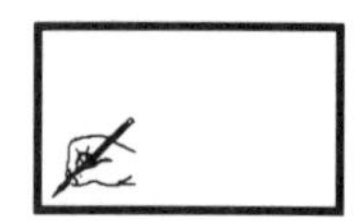

2. **Carry a small pocket notebook.** Write notes to yourself all day!
   - Dates
   - Messages

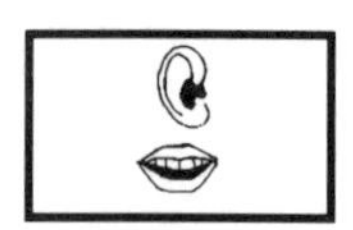

3. **Repeat the information over and over.** Repeating the information signals the brain that it is important to remember.
   - Ask yourself questions.
   - Discuss it with yourself.
   - Spell out words you need to remember.

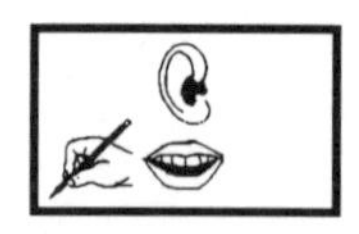

4. **React with emotion!**

   People usually remember things they have strong feelings about.

5. **Take good notes during a lecture.**

   Read the strategies for taking notes in Question F of this chapter.

   - Read your notes within 12 hours of taking them. You can add to them and clear up inconsistencies.

     If you wait too long before reading them, you won't be able to recall as much from the lecture.

   - Read your notes every night to put the information into your long-term memory.

     Reading them often signals the brain that they're important to remember.

D.

How can I concentrate on what a speaker is saying?

"Concentration" means the ability to focus on the center of attention (the speaker). You must learn to think only about what you are listening to.

1. Choose your seat carefully.

By choosing a good seat, you'll eliminate many distractions.

- Sit where you can see the speaker.
- Sit away from windows and doors.
- Sit away from the aisles so people don't walk by you.
- Sit by quiet people who won't talk while you are trying to listen.

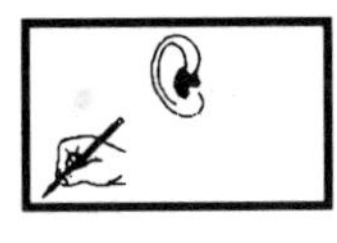

2. Watch and listen to the speaker carefully. Certain actions signal that important information is being given. Write down what he is saying when these things occur:

The speaker gives you signals when he wants you to pay very close attention to what he is saying. The information given when these changes occur is usually found on tests.

- His voice gets louder or softer.
- He stands up or straightens.
- He writes on the blackboard.
- He glances at his notes.
- He uses his hands and arms.
- He talks more slowly or more rapidly.
- He repeats information.
- He gives several examples.
- He tells you to remember it.
- He uses key phrases such as:

  "I can't emphasize enough..."
  "The most important event was..."
  "Two points to remember are..."
  "You will need to know..."

3. **Write down anything the teacher numbers.** Lists, steps, and sequences signal good test items.

Number one...
The first point is...
A, B, and C are...

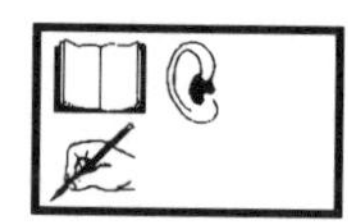

4. **Read the assignment before the lecture.** Most teachers will add new information to what you've read. Listen for it and write it down.

The material will sound familiar, so you won't be lost.

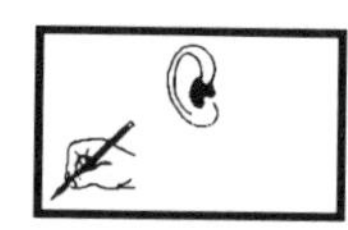

5. **Write fast and listen closely during the last 10 minutes of class!**

A teacher will often rush through important information so he can cover everything on his lesson plans for that day.

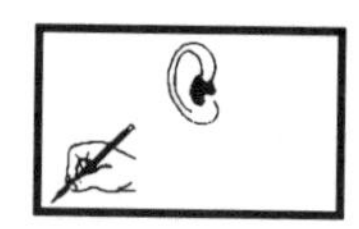

6. **Write down words and phrases during discussions and meetings.** Writing while you are listening makes you pay closer attention to what is being said.

This is called "pencil listening." You are programming yourself to listen.

7. **Ask yourself questions about what is being said.** Questioning will keep your mind active and thinking about what the speaker is saying.

"What is the reason for that?"
"Does that make sense?"

E.

What can I do to better understand what a speaker means?

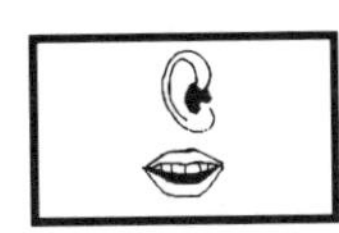

1. **Talk about your feelings on the topic.** How do you feel when you hear this subject mentioned?
   - Interested or bored?
   - Angry or indifferent?

Understanding your reactions will help you put your feelings aside as you focus on the speaker.

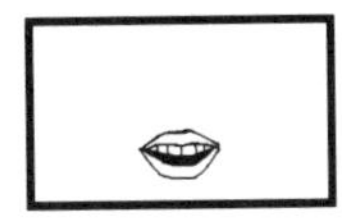

2. **Ask yourself what you already know** about the topic.

This "warms up" the brain to connect new information with what you already know.

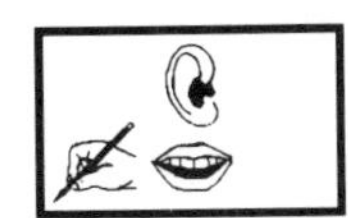

3. **Ask yourself questions** during the lecture.

   A. Write a question and leave a blank space after it for the answer.

   What caused that rebellion? ________

   B. Write the answer down when you hear it.

   If you don't hear the answer, ask someone or look it up.

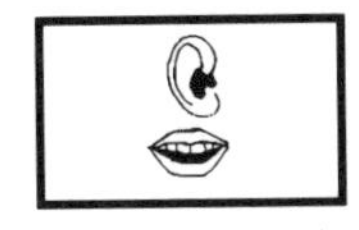

4. **Ask the speaker to repeat anything you don't understand.** He will usually word it in a different way.

You will probably understand it the second time.

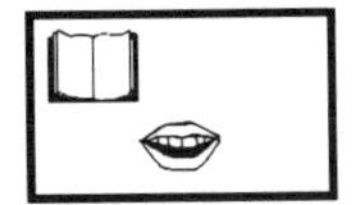

5. **Ask the speaker to write the information** on the blackboard. Do this for anything you don't understand.

He will usually explain further while he is writing.

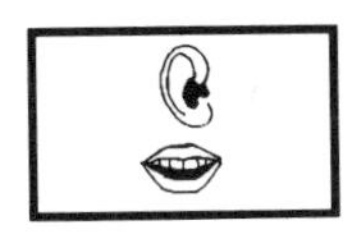

6. **Ask yourself what the speaker is really saying.** Is the teacher hinting at something without really saying it?

This is called "listening between the lines."

7. **Discuss the information with someone else from the class.** Compare notes while you are discussing the information.

- Discuss questions you have.
- Clear up misunderstandings.
- Fill in notes you have missed.

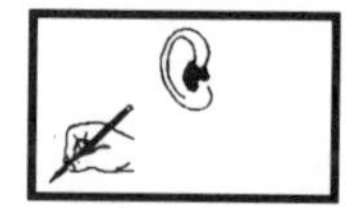

8. **Diagram the information as you listen.** The diagram below is an example.

   A. Write the broad topic in a circle.

   B. Write main ideas on lines coming out of the circle.

   C. Write facts and details on lines coming off the main idea lines.

Add to your diagram when you are studying your notes or when you are reading the textbook.

You may end up with many diagrams if he is presenting many main ideas.

Broad topic
Main idea
fact
fact
detail
Main idea
detail
Main idea
detail
fact
Main idea
detail
detail
fact

F.

How can I take good notes during a lecture?

1. **Keep a separate notebook for each subject.** Keep together:
   - All notes
   - Returned quizzes and tests
   - Assignments and returned papers
   - Handouts

Read Chapter 3: Question F: "How can I organize my class materials?"

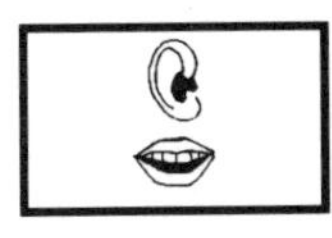

2. **Set a purpose for listening** before the lecture. Ask yourself review questions about the assignment, so you will be ready to listen.

The teacher will usually start lecturing from where he left off and from the reading he assigned.

3. **Date your notes.** This will help you to locate a certain page easily.

Teachers often refer to material they covered in previous lectures.

4. **Use speedwriting.** Develop your own "code" so you can take notes faster.

You can clear up any words you might have questions about later. Read your notes within 12 hours, while you still remember what was said.

- You can use:
  initials (JFK)
  abbreviations (TX)
  numerals and symbols
  (= for equals, w/o for without)

- You can leave out:
  most vowels (ppl=people)
  little words (an, the)
  ends of words (abbrev.)

The assassination of President John Kennedy on November 22, 1963, in Dallas, Texas, touched the lives of people all over the world.

JFK's assassination Dallas TX (11/22/63) touched ppl's lives all over world.

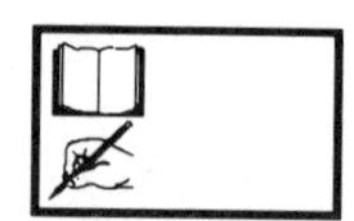

5. **Write main ideas close to the margin and indent supporting details.** While rereading or rewriting your notes, add the symbols used in outlining: Roman numerals, capital letters, numerals, and lowercase letters.

I. Speedwriting
  A. Initials
  B. Abbreviations
  C. Numerals
  D. Symbols
    1. = equals
    2. w/o without

6. **Don't worry about spelling.** Circle words you think are misspelled. Look them up later.

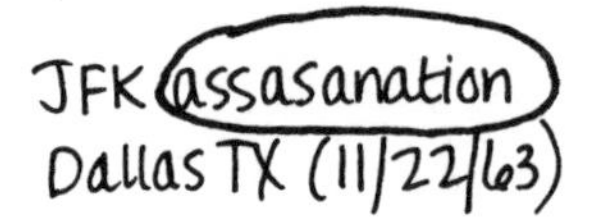

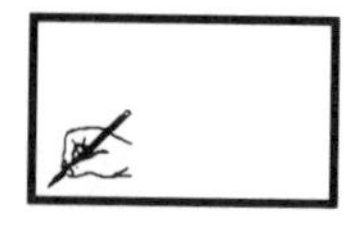

7. **Write important words and phrases in your notes if you're having trouble keeping up.** Leave a space after them. Fill in the information later when you have more time.

You'll at least end up with a rough outline that you can fill in later.

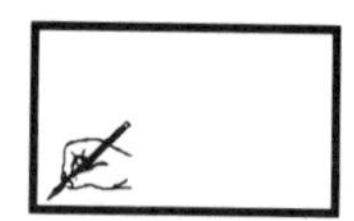

8. **Write a question mark (?) in the margin when you have missed information.** Leave a blank space after it to fill in later.

Also put a "?" where you don't understand something.

9. **Tape record the lecture.** Use a recorder that has a counter. When you don't understand something, put a "?" in your notes and write the counter number by the "?".

The counter number will tell you how far to rewind the tape to find the information. Example: tornado (?) #64

10. **Leave one page blank between each set of lecture notes.**

You will be able to add new information and still keep all of the information on that one topic together.

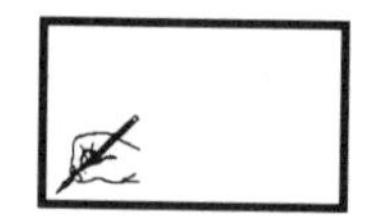

11. **Recopy your lecture notes.**

  A. Recopy them the same day you took them.

  You can add to them or clear up confusing points.

  B. Use highlighter pens to call attention to important points.

  They come in many colors and don't "bleed" through to the other side of the paper.

G.

How can I show a person I'm listening?

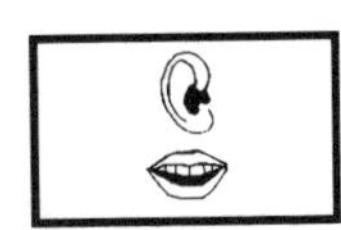

1. **Continue the same train of thought** when you respond to the speaker.

"Yes, I agree that a move is a big step."

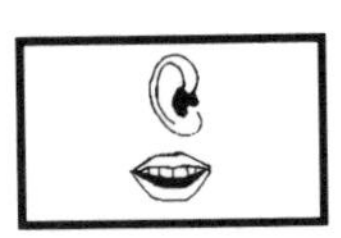

2. **Ask the person questions.** He knows you're listening if you ask questions.

"Will this be the last move you'll make for a while?"

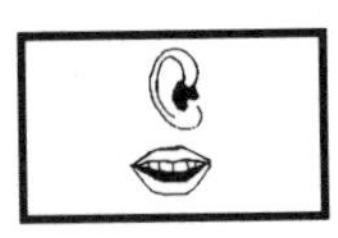

3. **Repeat what the other person has said** in your own words. Counselors often use this way of showing that they are listening.

"So you're saying that the kids are really excited about the move?"

4. **Use appropriate facial expressions** to respond to what the speaker is saying.

For example, smile if the speaker is happy.

5. **Use other appropriate nonverbal language.**

- Uncross arms and legs. — This shows openness.
- Don't yawn or look at your watch. — You'll look bored.
- Don't sit with your hands folded. — This shows a closed mind.

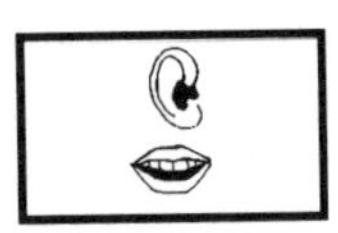

6. **Summarize what the person has said** before the conversation ends.

"So in just three months you'll be moving to France. How exciting!"

H.

What can I do to become a better listener?

A person learns to walk by walking, to cook by cooking, and to listen by listening. You need to practice to become a better listener.

1. **Test your listening skills using a professionally produced tape.** There are many books on tape you can work with.

   A. Write down test questions as you listen to an entire tape.

   B. Test yourself by answering the questions you made up.

   C. Check your answers by rewinding the tape and listening to it again.

Professional readers have:

- comfortable reading speed
- error-free pronunciation
- appropriate emotional tone

2. **Write sentences from a professionally produced tape.**

   A. Listen to one sentence. Push "pause."

   B. Write down what the sentence means. Release "pause."

   C. Rewind the tape to the beginning of that sentence.

   D. Listen to the sentence and compare it to the one you wrote down. Did you get the right meaning?

This is good practice for taking lecture notes.

When you are successful with one sentence, try two sentences.

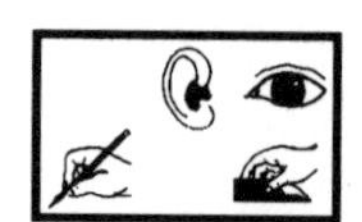

3. **Take notes from people speaking on TV.** Videotape the show you are transcribing, so you can check your notes for accuracy.

The more "live" dictation you take, the easier note-taking will become for you.

CHAPTER 6

Pronunciation and Accuracy in Reading

Being able to pronounce words quickly and accurately when you read is an important skill. If you recognize words easily, you can concentrate on the meaning of what you read. But if you spend a lot of effort figuring out how to pronounce words, you will have little energy left to comprehend what you read. This chapter gives you several strategies for learning how to pronounce words more quickly.

The chapter also contains strategies to help you overcome other problems that may be keeping you from reading faster and more easily. These problems include figuring out what words mean when you don't recognize them and losing your place on the page.

Read through the following statements. Sit back and think about each statement. Be honest! This is a personal survey, so it can only help you if you are honest about yourself.

Put a check mark in front of the statements that describe you:

____ A. I can't figure out what a word means when I don't recognize it.

____ B. I have trouble figuring out how to pronounce words quickly when I'm reading out loud.

____ C. I can't figure out how to pronounce words even when I have the time.

____ D. When I try to pronounce words, I add letters, omit letters, or change letters around.

____ E. I lose my place on the page while I am reading.

Choose the checked statement that is the most important to you at this time and note the letter to the right of your check mark. Turn to the section of this chapter that begins with that letter. Look for strategies that have the symbols for your preferred learning styles pictured in the left-hand column. Choose one of these strategies and follow the directions in the center column. Read the comments in the right-hand column for more hints. Try the strategy four or five times to see if it works for you. If it doesn't, try another. Strategies can be used individually or in combinations. Help yourself!

How can I figure out what a word means when I don't recognize it?

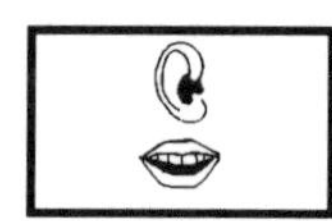

1. **Ask someone what a word means and how to pronounce it.** This is the fastest way.

It's a compliment to be asked, so people don't mind.

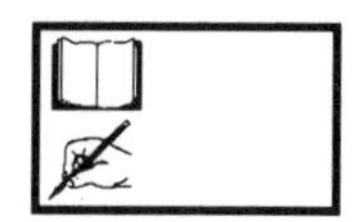

2. **Use context clues.**

"Context" means words that come before and after the unknown word.

A. Skip the unknown word and read the whole sentence. Then go back and see if you can figure out what the unknown word means by the words that come before and after it.

"I prefer *utilitarian* cars like the Jeep."

B. Write the unknown word on a blank strip of paper you can use as a bookmark. After you have tried to figure out the meaning using the context clues, look it up to see if you were right.

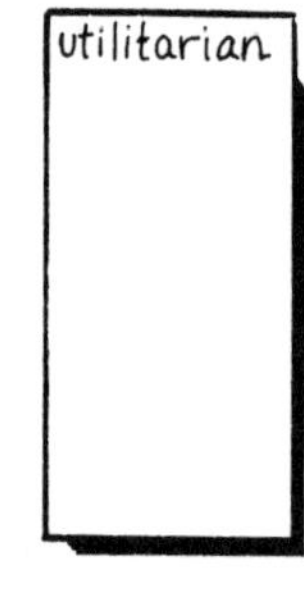

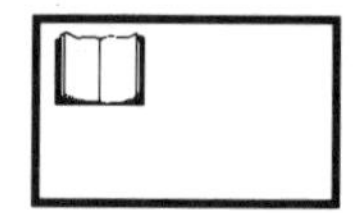

3. **Look for help from the author** when using context clues. Authors sometimes help readers understand difficult words by providing:

- synonyms (words with similar meanings)

  "The exercise is beneficial, or good, for his legs."

- explanations

  "The cat is nocturnal, so it's up all night."

- examples

  "I prefer utilitarian cars like the Jeep."

- definitions

  "An afghan is a knitted blanket."

4. **Make a list of highlighted vocabulary words and their meanings** before you start reading.

   A. Figure out the ways the author highlights vocabulary words.

   - Bold or italicized print
   - Vocabulary words in margin
   - Lists at the beginning or end of chapter

   B. Write the vocabulary words on a blank strip of paper you can use as a bookmark. Look up definitions you aren't sure of. These two resources can help:

   Keep this in the chapter, so you will see it often.

   - Glossary: a list of a book's difficult words and their meanings.

   Found at the back of the book

   - Dictionary: complete resource for word definitions.

   Always keep a dictionary in your work area.

5. **Use a dictionary.** There are two steps in using a dictionary:

   A. Open to the section the word is likely to be found in.

   "cat" = beginning section
   "mouse" = middle section
   "vine" = last section

   B. Use the guide words. You are on the right page if the word you're looking for falls alphabetically between the two guide words.

   - Left-hand corner: first word on that page
   - Right-hand corner: last word on that page

6. **Use an electronic dictionary.** Simply type in the word. The meanings will appear on the screen.

   Some electronic dictionaries will also pronounce the word.

B.

How can I figure out how to pronounce words quickly when I'm reading out loud?

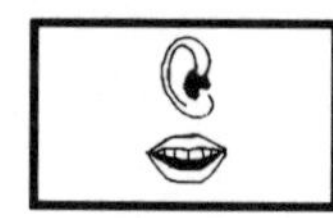

1. **Discuss your pronunciation problems with your teacher.** She will need to consider:

   - The difficulty of the reading material for you.
   - Whether or not she should call on you. She can choose not to call on you, or give you the option to say "pass."

"I really get nervous when I have to read out loud because I can't figure out how to pronounce all the words."

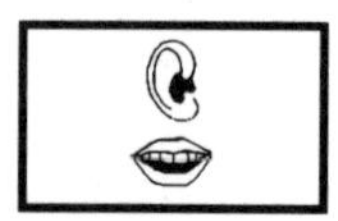

2. **Ask someone sitting near you for help.** Ask her to whisper the word to you if you hesitate while you're reading out loud.

People like to help out and don't mind being asked.

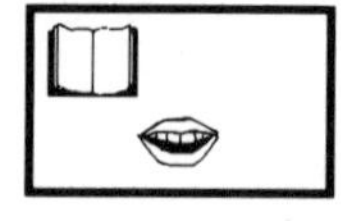

3. **Read more slowly when reading out loud.** This will buy you time to figure out how to pronounce words.

A beginning pianist uses one of the pedals to buy herself time to figure out the notes.

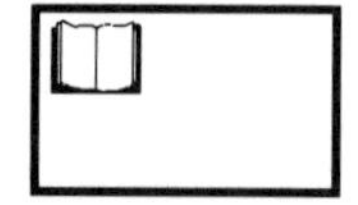

4. **Look for parentheses ( ) following the word.** Pronunciation is often shown in parentheses.

atria (ay tree uh)

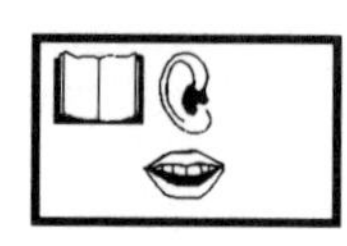

5. **See if the word is a compound word.** Long words are often made up of two individual words. Pronounce them separately and then together.

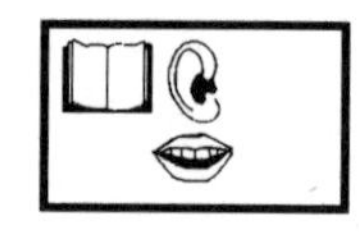

6. **Say the parts of the word you know.** The pronunciation of the entire word will often "click" when you hear yourself say the familiar parts.

com/bust = combust
con/nec/tion = connection
super/abundant = superabundant

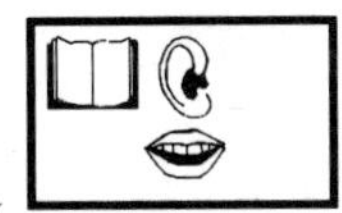

7. **Say the word in a whisper** before you say it out loud. You will be able to tell if it sounds right.

Your *listening* vocabulary is much larger than your *reading* vocabulary. You'll know when it sounds right.

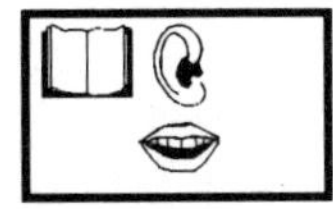

8. **Look for a suffix at the end of words.** Sometimes when a suffix is added to a word, the accent changes so the word is pronounced differently.

method*ical*	me/thod'/i/cal
human*ity*	hu/man'/i/ty
metal*lic*	me/tal'/lic

C.

How can I figure out how to pronounce words even when I have the time?

1. **Read along with a professionally produced tape to practice pronunciation.** Ask for books that have read-along tapes at your local school or city library.

   A. Write down unfamiliar words on a blank strip of paper you can use as a bookmark. Look up the meanings when you have more time.

   B. Write the page number and counter number alongside the word. You will be able to find the word again quickly in the book or on the tape.

You will also be practicing a comfortable reading speed.

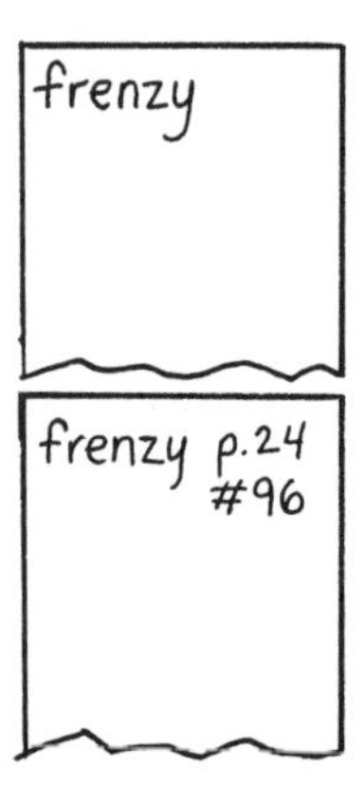

2. **Play Scrabble™ and other word games.** These games will increase your awareness of word parts and introduce you to new words that other players use.

Write down any unfamiliar words other people use and look them up later.

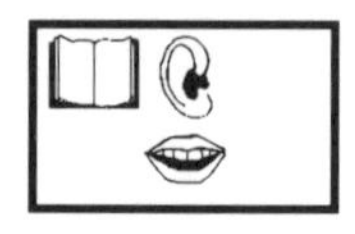

3. **See if the word is a compound word.** Two individual words are often combined to make one long word. Pronounce them separately and then together.

breeze/way = breezeway

4. **Learn how to pronounce prefixes** (word elements that carry meaning and are attached to the beginning of root words). If you can pronounce the prefix, you can already pronounce part of the word.

   - Say the prefix out loud. Then read the word.
   - Write the word and underline the prefix. Say the word out loud.

Use the prefix list in the appendix at the back of this book to practice pronouncing prefixes.

"*pre-* preschool"
"*mis-* misdeed"

transform
hydropower

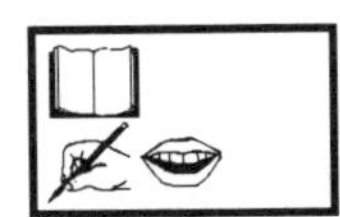

5. Learn how to pronounce suffixes (word elements that carry meaning and are attached to the end of root words). If you can pronounce the suffix, you can already pronounce part of the word.

Use the suffix list in the appendix at the back of this book to practice pronouncing suffixes.

- Say the suffix out loud. Then read the word.

"*-ment* payment"
"*-ful* insightful"

- Write the word and underline the suffix. Say the word out loud.

harmless
pitcher

General Tip: **If you have trouble pronouncing long words,** use the word lists in the appendix at the back of this book.

There are separate lists of words containing:

- short vowels
- long vowels
- other vowel sounds
- silent consonants
- prefixes
- roots
- suffixes

Play Scrabble™ and other word games.

D.

What can I do about adding, omitting, changing, or substituting letters or words when I read?

Some people have trouble reading words exactly as they appear on the page. The errors they make can change the meaning of what they read. Imagine how confusing it would be to misread the words "crate it" as "create it" or "cremate it."

The first step in dealing with this problem is becoming aware of what changes you are making. Use the following strategies to spot errors. Then pay careful attention to those areas whenever you read or write.

General Tip: **Write this checklist on an index card.** Use it to figure out the types of errors you make. Awareness is the key; you can't correct something you aren't aware of.

- Add endings
- Add letters
- Add words
- Substitute different words
- Leave off endings
- Leave out letters
- Leave out words

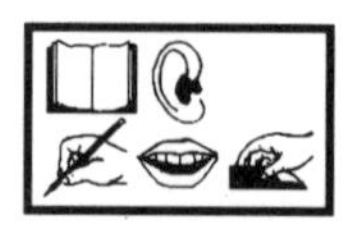

1. **Read into a tape recorder** to find the errors you are making.

   A. Read a paragraph from one of your books. Use your normal reading speed.

   Keep reading paragraphs and check off any changes until you see a pattern developing.

   B. Rewind the tape. Listen to the paragraph you recorded as you read along in the book. Whenever you have made an error in your taped reading, mark it on your checklist.

   "My main problem area is endings. I'll have to watch endings from now on."

   C. Circle the categories in which you have the most check marks.

   Watch these places while you are reading!

2. Change your reading speed. This time read paragraphs into the tape recorder more slowly. Chart any errors you make by following the steps in Tip 1.

- Are you making the same errors?
- Are you making fewer errors when you read more slowly?

E.

How can I keep my place on a page while I am reading?

These strategies should be used only when you are having trouble keeping your place on the page.

1. **Glide your finger under the words** as you are reading them. Keep your finger moving.

Your speed will increase as you get used to "finger reading."

2. **Put your finger on the side of the page** at the end of the sentence you are reading. As you reach the end of the line, move your finger down to the next line.

You will always know which line you are on.

3. **Put a bookmark under the sentence you are reading.** Move it down the page as you read. You can use an "L"-shaped or rectangular-shaped bookmark.

This focuses your attention directly on the sentence you are reading.

4. **Place a 4" x 6" index card under the sentence you are reading** to block out the rest of the page. Keep moving it down as you come to the end of the line.

Your eyes won't jump ahead.

5. **Hold a pencil in your writing hand.** Put it at one end of the line you are reading. Keep it moving down the page as you are reading.

Use the eraser end of the pencil, so you don't make marks when you "pencil track."

6. **Place a piece of paper above the line you are reading.** Keep moving it down the page as you read.

You will always know which line you are reading and your eyes won't jump around.

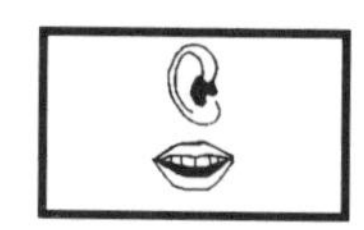

7. **Read out loud.**

This will help you if you learn best by listening and speaking.

CHAPTER 7

Reading Comprehension

Reading comprehension is the act of understanding what you read. When you comprehend, you get meaning out of what you read.

Successful readers are as alert when they read as when they drive a car. When driving, you're continually made aware of how you're doing and what you need to do next by what is going on around you. Speed limit signs tell you when you need to slow down. Street signs can let you know that you've made a wrong turn.

When you read, however, you are not always given signals to tell you when you don't understand something, when you need to slow down, or when you have mistaken one word for another word. You must learn to alert yourself to these problems, so you can make the adjustments that are needed.

Read the following statements about the area of reading comprehension. Sit back and think about each statement. Be honest! This is your personal survey, so it can only help you if you are honest about yourself.

Put a check mark in front of the statements that describe you:

____ A. I don't know how fast or slowly I should read something.

____ B. I don't know how to prepare myself before I start to read.

____ C. I have trouble understanding the material while I am reading.

____ D. I forget what I've read after a short time.

____ E. I miss the main ideas when I read.

____ F. I have trouble understanding what I've read.

____ G. I don't take good notes while I am reading.

Choose the checked statement that is the most important to you at this time and note the letter to the right of your check mark. Turn to the section of this chapter that begins with that letter. Look for strategies that have the symbols for your preferred learning styles pictured in the left-hand column. Choose one of these strategies and follow the directions in the center column. Read the comments in the right-hand column for more hints. Try the strategy four or five times to see if it works for you. If it doesn't, try another. Strategies can be used individually or in combinations. Help yourself!

What affects how fast or slowly I should read something?

Before you can decide how fast or slowly you need to read something, there are three things to consider: 1) your purpose for reading, 2) the difficulty of the material, and 3) how well you know the subject matter. All these factors play a part in how fast you should read something. Look at the chart on page 89. Whether you're reading for study or pleasure, the chart suggests various appropriate reading rates.

1. **Decide what your purpose is in reading.**

   - Skimming should be done when you need to find a particular word or answer. It is done quickly by running your finger down the middle of the page and skimming both sides.

   - Technical books and textbooks should be read more slowly using reading strategies found in this chapter. You will be reading to understand and remember the information.

Decide how fast you will read before you start reading.
- What are you reading?
- Why are you reading it?

2. **Use the "hand test" for one page** to judge how difficult the reading is for you.

   A. Start reading at the top of the page and put up one finger every time you come to a word you don't know.

   B. If you put up five fingers before you get to the end of the page, the book will be difficult for you to read. If you decide to continue reading the book, schedule more time for your reading and use other strategies in this chapter.

The more difficult it is, the more slowly you need to read.

If you are reading purely for enjoyment, don't struggle with a book or magazine that's too difficult. Choose something else to read.

Reading Rates

Find the statement that describes your reading need and use the speed indicated to read most efficiently.

	Reading for Pleasure	Reading for Study
Slow Reading	Enjoy books, plays, articles, poetry, etc.	Learn content. Understand difficult materials.
Normal Reading	Read to remember material.	Understand material of average difficulty.
Fast Reading	Refresh your memory of material you've read before. Read for enjoyment rather than to remember.	Review material. Read to find specific pieces of information in text.
Skimming	Choose an interesting article or book to read. Locate a specific paragraph you've read before.	Find specific information in an index, glossary, table of contents, etc.

3. Estimate how much time you have for your reading.

- Novels can be read fast for enjoyment. If you are reading them to study characters, cause and effect, or other critical reading elements, you will need to schedule more time.

Read novels faster by stopping after each chapter to predict what will happen next. You will read faster to find out if you are right!

- If you don't have much time for reading your textbook:
  1. Read the first two sentences and the last two sentences of each paragraph.
  2. Turn headings into questions so you will know what to look for while reading.
  3. Skim the chapter to find out what is most important.

Main ideas are usually found in these two places.

Who? What? Why?
When? Where? How?

Pay attention to:
- Introduction
- Headings
- Numbers
- Summary
- Words in bold and italics

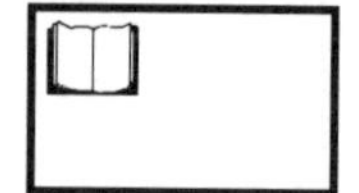

4. Practice these reading activities to increase your reading speed.

- Read! Read! Read! Push yourself to do a lot of reading.

The words will become more familiar, so you will be able to read faster.

- Read what you are interested in. You will read faster and this speed will transfer to your other reading.

• Magazines
• Comic books
• Sports books
• "How to" books

- Tell yourself how fast you will read. Push yourself to read a little faster than you are used to reading. Make yourself go from a "trot" to a "run"!

People often read slowly out of habit. They don't switch reading speeds.

- Carry a book around with you. You can read whenever you have some free time.

• Bus trips
• Waiting rooms
• Laundromats

- Read along with someone. You read one paragraph, and the other person reads the next one.

You will set a faster pace for each other than if you read alone.

B.

How can I prepare myself before I start to read?

General Tip: **Set a purpose for your reading.** Turn the headings into questions.

Read to find the answers to your questions.

1. **Talk about any feelings you already have about the topic.** What do you think of when you hear this subject mentioned?

Thinking about the topic ahead of time will get you ready to read about it.

2. **Write down what you already know about the topic.** This makes it easier for your brain to connect the new information to what is already stored knowledge.

Reviewing information about a topic before you start to read helps you understand it.

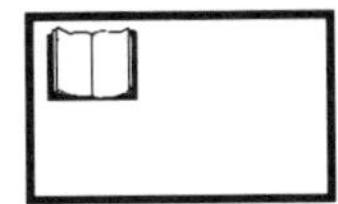

3. **Preview the book or chapter** to prepare yourself for what is coming.

- Book:
  - Title
  - Author
  - Publication date
  - Table of contents
  - Appendices
  - Glossary
  - Index

Publication dates are especially important in subjects that change rapidly, such as science.

- Chapter:
  - Title
  - Introduction
  - Headings
  - Pictures, graphs and charts
  - Captions
  - Vocabulary
  - Summary
  - Review questions

You need to warm up your body before sporting events or aerobics. You need to warm up your brain before it is "hit" with a lot of new information!

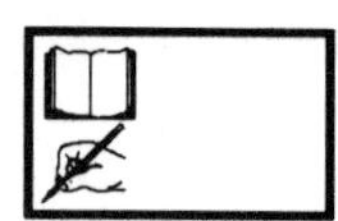

4. **Make a skeletal outline.** Use the information you gained from skimming the chapter or book.

   A. Write down headings from your textbook, lecture notes, handouts, and study guides.

   B. Leave large blank areas under each heading for your notes.

   C. When you start reading, you will take notes under the appropriate headings.

5. **Make a "map" of the chapter** using the chapter title, headings, and subheadings.

This gives you an overview of the chapter's structure.

Chapter Title

Heading 1 — Subhead, Subhead, Subhead

Heading 2 — Subhead, Subhead

Heading 3 — Subhead, Subhead

C.

How can I improve my comprehension while reading?

1. Read with a pen or pencil in your hand. Write down what you are thinking and what is important while you are reading.

Make yourself "a part" of the book, not "apart" from it.

- Write down questions in the margins of the book (if you own it) or on a large, blank piece of paper you can use as a bookmark.

Then read to find the answers to your questions.

- Circle or make a list of words that are in bold or italic print or write them on your bookmark. Find out what makes these words important.

Bold or italic print points out important words and ideas.

- Write down your comments.
  - Do you agree or disagree?
  - Is there a relationship between two things or ideas?

Look for answers to these comments as you are reading.

- Write the main point of the paragraph in the margin or on your bookmark.

Just write a few words or phrases that will remind you of the main point.

2. Make a study guide while you are reading. A study guide will help you to understand and remember specialized vocabulary. Often it is this vocabulary that is getting in the way of your understanding the material.

Read Question G, Tip 4, in this chapter on making study guides.

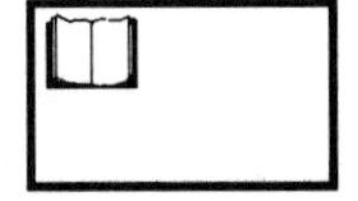

3. Make predictions. As you come to each new chapter or section, try to predict what it will be about.

Read to find out if you are right.

4. Turn each major heading into a question. Write down each question. Read to find the answer.

The Cell Wall
What makes up a cell wall?

5. Use a tape recorder. When you come to a part you don't understand, read it into the tape recorder. Play it back, so you can hear it read to you.

Hearing something often helps you understand it.

6. Visualize what you are reading. Close your eyes and pretend you are seeing the information in a movie. Try to "see" every detail and every person you have read about.

A picture is worth a thousand words. Study the illustrations to help you visualize.

7. Ask someone what something means. Hearing it explained in a different way often helps you understand it.

Call someone who is studying the same thing and ask him to explain it.

8. Use context clues to figure out what a word means.

"The toga covered the Roman's body from shoulder to ankle."

A. Skip the word and read the rest of the sentence.

"The_____ covered the Roman's body from shoulder to ankle."

B. Read the whole sentence again and try to figure out what the word means by the words that come before and after it.

(The words after "toga" tell us that it must be some kind of clothing.)

9. Use a dictionary to look up the meaning or pronunciation of important words.

The glossary at the back of a textbook defines words that are used in it.

10. Pay attention to the room you're reading in. Is it helping you to concentrate on your reading?

Does it match the environment you work well in? See Chapter 2.

11. Stop any rhythmic activities. They slow your reading down.

- Moving head?
- Tapping pencil?

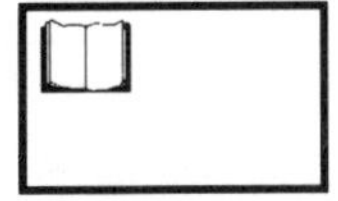

12. Pay attention to transition words. Look at the chart on page 96 for some transition words and what they signal.

They signal some sort of change.

If you are having trouble understanding what you are reading, read it into a tape recorder. Then play it back so you can hear it. Hearing something often helps you understand it.

Transition Words

These expressions are used to describe relationships.

first
meanwhile
then
in the end
later
soon
now
immediately
while
at that point
when
whenever
as
presently
until
finally
after
afterward
formerly
at once
at last
in the meantime

These expressions are used to describe where an object or person is.

outside
inside
beyond
below
nearby
near
behind
beside
next to
above
here
there
to the right
to the left
in the distance
across from
also
besides
then
again

These expressions are used to demonstrate a cause-and-effect relationship.

consequently
as a result
therefore
thus
to this end

These expressions are used to offer a choice.

otherwise
neither...nor
instead of
on the other hand
either...or

These expressions are used to describe a contrast between two or more things.

although
however
while
yet
but
unlike
whereas
conversely
still
rather than
on the other hand
in contrast to
more than
less than
instead of

These expressions are used to show that something is being added to what was already said.

at last
both...and
another
likewise
next
finally
then too
moreover
most importantly
furthermore
in addition
equally important
first, second, third...

These expressions are used to emphasize what is being said.

in fact
certainly
clearly, then
indeed
of course
obviously
truly

These expressions are used to make a comparison.

similarly
as...as
like
both...and
likewise
in the same way

These expressions are used to summarize material.

accordingly
in conclusion
therefore
for these reasons
to summarize

These expressions are used to introduce an example.

thus
for example
for instance

D.

What can I do after I have read something in order to remember it?

1. Say the information out loud as you write it. Then visualize the information in your mind's eye. Repeat these steps. Repetition is the key to remembering.

Use as many of your senses as you can. Read it. Write it. Say it. Listen to it. Visualize it. Manipulate it.

2. Use a tape recorder.

A. Dictate what you have to remember.

1. Read the information. Count to five silently.
2. Read the answer. Count to five silently.

"H_2O"
1-2-3-4-5

"water"
1-2-3-4-5

B. Take the self-test review.

1. Listen to the tape. Push "pause."
2. Write or say the answer. Let up "pause."
3. Listen to the answer and check it against the one you have given.

H_2O =

"water"

3. Make flash cards.

Read Chapter 4: Question E on flash cards

- Write the term on one side, the definition on the other side.
- Write the question on one side, the answer on the other side.
- Write the date on one side, the event on the other side.

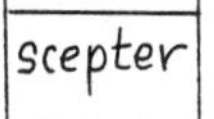

staff of authority

What is a stylus?

A sharp tool

1492

Columbus discovered America

E.

How can I find the main idea?

Paragraphs in textbooks often contain main idea statements. These general statements are usually located in the first, second, or last sentence of the paragraph. The rest of the paragraph usually contains details and examples to support the main idea.

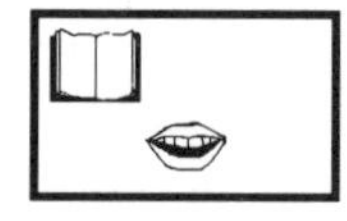

1. **Stop after the first two sentences of a paragraph.** Ask yourself what it said.

The first sentence is the most likely place to find the main idea.

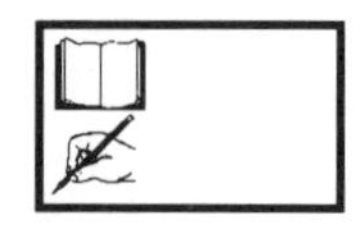

2. **Read the last sentence of the paragraph.** Is the main idea there?

The last sentence is the second most likely place to find the main idea.

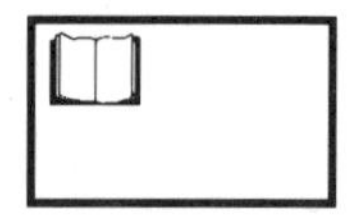

3. **Turn the heading of each section into a question.** The main idea will be found by answering this question. Write down the question and your answer.

Fact vs. Opinion
"What is the difference between fact and opinion?"

4. **Work with another person** to practice finding the main idea.

   A. Read the same paragraph.

   B. Check to see if you agree on the main idea.

   C. If you disagree, ask a third person which main idea he agrees with.

Work with someone who is good at this skill, or it won't help you.

F.

What can I do after I have read something in order to understand it?

1. **Diagram what you have read.** You will be able to see relationships and remember the information. You can visualize your diagram to "see" it in your mind's eye.

Succession to the Presidency
President
Vice President
Speaker of the House
President Pro Tempore of Senate

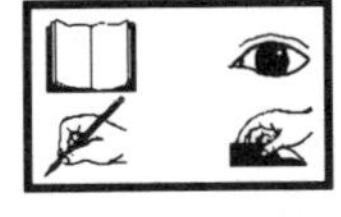

2. **Mark your notes.**

   A. Use different colored pens: one color for lecture notes and another color for textbook notes.

   Lecture notes = blue
   Book notes = black

   B. Color code your notes. Use different colors to:

   This will help you find important points more quickly.

   - Circle vocabulary words.
   - Underline facts.
   - Circle numerals.
   - Put a question mark by anything you don't understand, or in places where you are missing information.
   - Write a numeral in the margin to tell you how many points you need to remember.

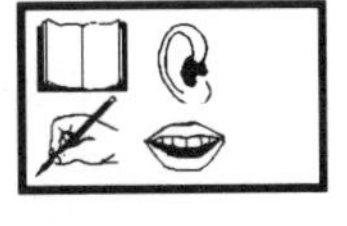

3. **Write the answers to questions found at the end of sections or the end of the chapter.** The author put them there to draw your attention to the main points. If you learn best by listening or speaking, give your answers out loud instead of writing them.

The questions will help you focus on what is important in the chapter.

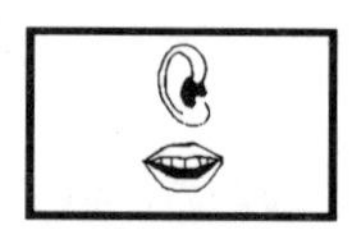

4. **Talk to someone else about your reading.**

New or different ideas will help you understand your reading.

5. **Map out information** to give yourself a visual picture. Seeing what you have read makes it easier to understand.

A good way to reinforce what you've read is to make a chapter "map." The map below, based on a chapter about the Civil War, is a good example.

The Civil War

Causes	Battles	Important People
Slavery	Gettysburg	Ulysses S. Grant
Economics	Antietam	Frederick Douglass
Cultural Differences	Bull Run	Abraham Lincoln
		Robert E. Lee

G.

How can I take good notes on what I read?

1. **Keep a separate notebook for each subject.** In it, you can keep together:
   - Notes
   - Returned quizzes and tests
   - Handouts

Read Chapter 3: Question F: "How can I organize my class materials?"

2. **Write only on the top half of each page or use only the front of each piece of notebook paper.** This will enable you to add new information and still keep everything on that topic together.

Add new information in a different color ink so you know whether it came from the lecture or textbook.

3. **Use speedwriting** to take notes quickly.

Use:
- initials (U.S.A.)
- abbreviations (Am)
- numerals and symbols (= for equals, w/o for without)

4. **Make a study guide as you read.** There are three different types of study guides.
   - ***Line study guide***. Write the fact (or question) on one line and the answer below it.
   - ***Vertical study guide***. Draw a line down your paper. Put the fact (or question) to the left of the line. Put the answer to the right of the line.
   - ***Outline study guide***.
     Roman numerals: headings of chapter.
     Capital letters: subheadings
     Numerals: details about the subheadings

1. Eli Whitney
   invented cotton gin
2. Thomas Edison
   invented electric light
   invented phonograph

Eli Whitney	cotton gin
Thomas Edison	electric light phonograph

I. Inventors
   A. Eli Whitney
      1. cotton gin
   B. Thomas Edison
      1. electric light
      2. phonograph

- All of these study guides have one thing in common: You can cover up one part of the guide so you can quiz yourself. Try this procedure for taking a self-quiz:
    1. Cover part of the guide.
    2. Question yourself out loud.
    3. Give your answer.
    4. Move the paper to check your answer.

Cover the answer side the first time you study it. Then cover the question side and ask yourself what question would go with that answer. You need to be ready to answer the questions both ways.

CHAPTER 8

Writing

Writing is often the only communication you will have with another person or company. What will your writing say about you? Will it give the impression of an educated, articulate, neat person, or of a sloppy person who can't express herself well? If you do not develop your writing skills, you might give an entirely false picture of yourself.

We use writing in our daily lives as well as in most jobs. We write notes to ourselves and notes to our family. We make up grocery lists, and fill out checks, order forms, and application forms. We also write personal letters and business letters. Each person's situation and writing needs are different. We must remember, however, that all writing must express what we want to say in a clear, understandable way. The strategies in this chapter can help you improve your writing, especially in terms of spelling, organization, and appearance.

Read through the following statements that deal with writing. Sit back and think about each statement. Be honest! This is a personal survey, so it can only help if you are honest about yourself!

Put a check mark in front of the statements that describe you:

____ A. I rearrange or reverse letters when I write them.

____ B. I don't know what to do about poor spelling while I am writing.

____ C. I am not a good speller.

____ D. I don't use interesting vocabulary in my writing.

____ E. I have trouble putting on paper what I want to say.

____ F. The appearance of my written work is poor.

Choose the checked statement that is the most important to you at this time and note the letter to the right of your check mark. Turn to the section of this chapter that begins with that letter. Look for strategies that have the symbols for your preferred learning styles pictured in the left-hand column. Choose one of these strategies and follow the directions in the center column. Read the comments in the right-hand column for more hints. Try the strategy four or five times to see if it works for you. If it doesn't, try another. Strategies can be used individually or in combinations. Help yourself!

A.

What can I do if I rearrange or reverse letters when I write them?

Some people have difficulty writing because they often rearrange or reverse letters. For example, they may write *was* when they mean *saw*, or write *b* when they mean *d*. The strategies below can help eliminate these writing errors.

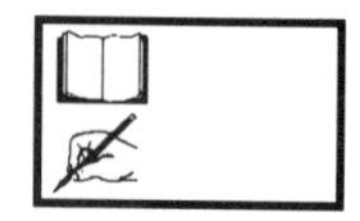

1. **Make a list of your "problem letters."** Whenever you reverse or rearrange letters, write them down.

Once you know which letters give you trouble, you can take more care when writing them.

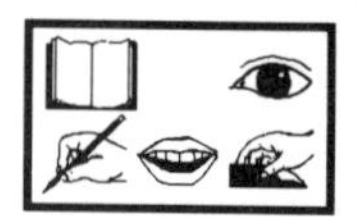

2. **Practice these four steps with each of your "problem letters."**

   A. Write the letter at the top of the paper. This will be your "guide letter."

   B. Say the letter out loud while you trace it with your pencil or pen.

   C. Close your eyes and visualize it. "See" it with your mind's eye.

   D. Write the letter without looking at it. Check what you have written with the "guide letter."

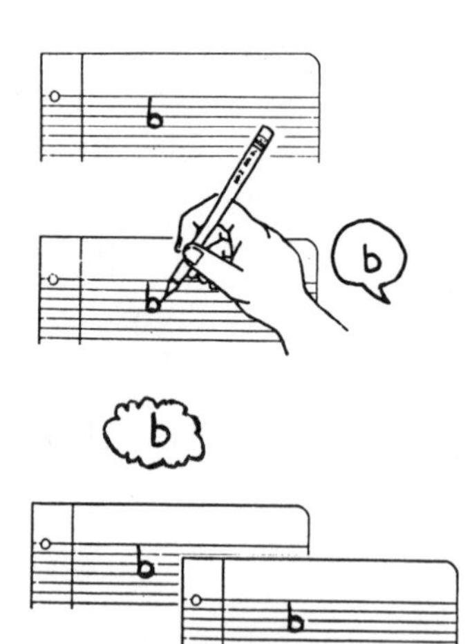

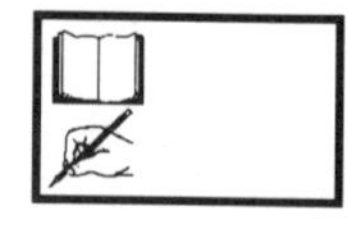

3. **Write 10 words that contain the "problem letter."** Underline that letter in each word.

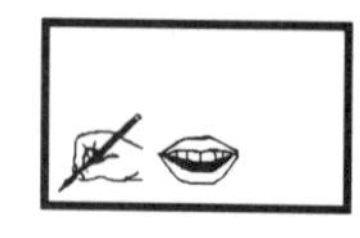

4. **Make up a mnemonic to help you remember the letter.** A mnemonic is a "memory jogger," something that helps you remember. Write the word while you say the mnemonic out loud.

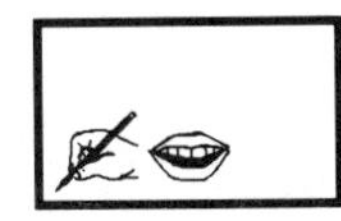

5. **Say the letter combination out loud** as you write it, if you rearrange letters.

For example, if you tend to write *shcool* for *school* say "s-c-h" out loud as you write it.

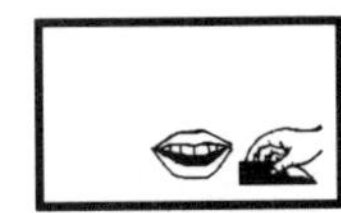

6. **Take a keyboarding class.** Say the letters to yourself and look at them as they appear on the computer screen.

This will help you connect the name of the letter with what it looks like.

7. **Play computer games!** They involve constant repetition in up/down and left/right movements.

You'll improve your eye-hand coordination, which will help your writing.

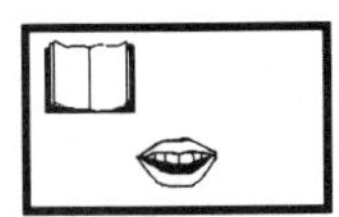

8. **Always proofread your written work.**

   A. The first time you read it, check for your problem letters and letter combinations.

   Look only for these letters the first time.

   B. The second time you read it, check the spelling of all words. It may help to read it out loud.

   Check any spellings you are unsure of in the dictionary.

General Tip: **Give all of your attention to your writing.**

Don't talk! Don't watch TV! Don't eat!

B.

What are some quick ways to correct my spelling while writing?

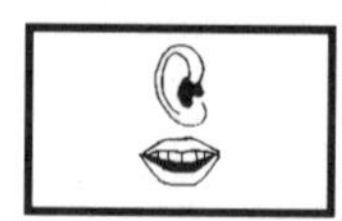

1. **Ask people around you how to spell the word.**

It's a lot faster than using the dictionary.

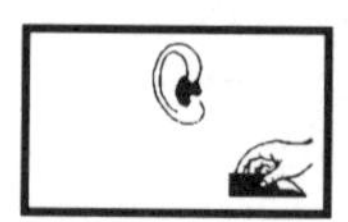

2. **Use a typewriter that has a spelling alert.** A sound will alert you to an error in spelling.

This frees you up to write words you use when talking, but you are not sure how to spell.

3. **Keep a dictionary handy.** Different sizes are available for different locations.

   - Keep a larger desk-size in your study area.
   - Get a pocket-size dictionary to carry with you.
   - Try a quick-reference pocket-size dictionary that contains only the spelling and how to divide the word. It doesn't give definitions.

You can also buy a "bad speller's" dictionary. They are designed for people who have trouble with spelling.

4. **Use an electronic dictionary.** Type in the word the way you think it is spelled. A list of correctly spelled words will appear on the screen, and you can select the right word.

It's much faster than using a traditional dictionary.

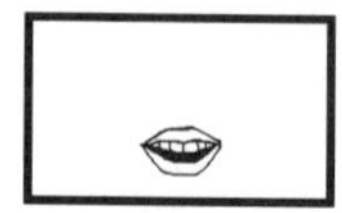

5. **Ask someone to proofread your paper when it's done.** Make sure that person is an excellent speller.

"Would you please check this for spelling errors? I'd appreciate it."

C.

How can I improve my spelling?

1. **Buy a "bad speller's" dictionary.** These dictionaries list words in alphabetical order by their common misspellings. Look up the word the way you think it is spelled. The dictionary will give you the correct spelling.

You are more likely to look up a word if a dictionary is handy. Carry it in your purse, glove compartment, briefcase, or backpack.

2. **Buy an electronic dictionary or speller.** You can type the word the way you think it is spelled. A list of correctly spelled words will appear on the screen, and you can select the right word.

They are much faster to use than a traditional dictionary.

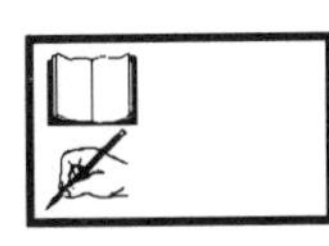

3. **Study words to find connections between the words and what they mean.** Write the words and underline the letters that go together.

h<u>ear</u> = <u>ear</u>

<u>here</u> = t<u>here</u>

4. **Write the prefixes and suffixes as you say them out loud.** When you know how to spell the beginnings and endings of words, you will only have to figure out how to spell the root words.
   - Prefix: a word element that carries meaning and is attached to the beginning of a root word.
   - Suffix: a word element that carries meaning and is attached to the end of a root word.

Use the lists of prefixes and suffixes in the appendix at the back of this book to practice writing them correctly.

For example: <u>auto</u>graph

For example: voice<u>less</u>

5. **Write a spelling test for yourself.** Have someone read it to you until you can spell the words correctly five days in a row.

Try making up a test that contains at least 10 words.

6. Use a tape recorder to study spelling.

A. Record your words on tape:

1. Read a word out loud. Count to five silently.
2. Spell the word out loud one letter at a time. Count to five silently.

"occasion"
1-2-3-4-5

"o-c-c-a-s-i-o-n"
1-2-3-4-5

B. Take the spelling test:

1. Listen to the word. Push "pause."
2. Write the word. Release "pause."
3. Listen to the answer. Check it against the one you have written.

occasion (push pause)

7. Make a list of words you often misspell. Use a small notebook and set aside one page for each letter of the alphabet. Put all your "problem words" that begin with *a* on the A page, *b* words on the B page, etc. You can include:

- Misspelled words from classwork
- Words from your personal writing you've had to look up in the dictionary

Keep the list in your study area, so you can practice them often.

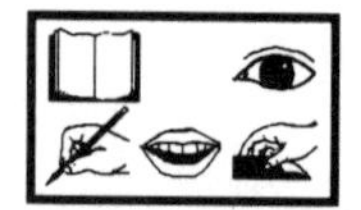

8. Practice your spelling with these five steps:

A. Read the word out loud.

B. Copy the word. Make sure you have spelled it correctly.

C. Spell it one letter at a time out loud. Trace it with your pen.

D. Visualize the word. Close your eyes and "see" it in your mind's eye.

E. Say the word out loud as you write it again. Check what you have written against the one you copied.

"occasion"

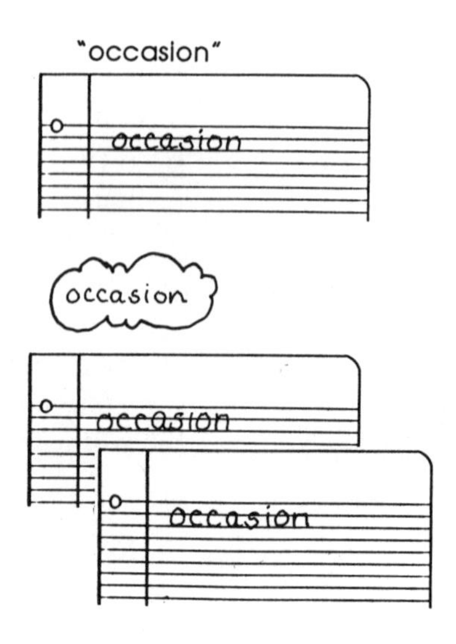

General Tip: **Learn basic spelling rules.** The chart below lists several basic rules. Read the spelling rules out loud. Write the example words as you think about the rules.

Basic Spelling Rules*

Rule	Example
Doubling Pattern 1: Double the final consonant if a word has one syllable, one vowel, and one final consonant, and the suffix starts with a vowel. Do not double *w* or x.	rip + ing = ripping pat + ed = patted fat + er = fatter
Silent *e* Pattern 1: Drop the silent *e* at the end of a word if the suffix begins with a vowel.	file + ing = filing adore + ed = adored rude + er = ruder
Silent *e* Pattern 2: Do not drop the silent *e* at the end of a word that ends in *ce* or *ge* if the suffix begins with an *a* or an *o*.	change + able = changeable
Changing y to i: When adding a suffix to a word that ends in *y*, change the *y* to *i* unless the suffix begins with *i*. After changing the *y* to *i*, add *es* instead of *s* to nouns and verbs.	berry + s = berries hairy + er = hairier scurry + ed = scurried
Doubling Pattern 2: If a word has more than one syllable, double the final consonant if the suffix starts with a vowel and the last syllable has one final vowel, one final consonant and is accented.	begin + ing = beginning

*Adapted from *Patterns in Spelling*, by Tim Brown and Deborah F. Knight. (New Readers Press, 1990)

D.

How can I use more interesting vocabulary in my writing?

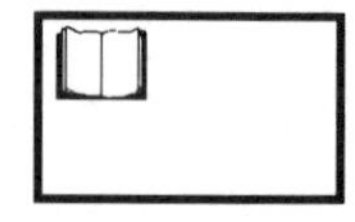

1. Use a thesaurus or synonym dictionary. These reference books give you a choice of many words to use in place of ones you have used over and over again.

Keep them handy in your work area.

2. Increase your vocabulary by:

- Reading a lot. You will begin to use new words without thinking about them because you have seen them so often.

Read anything that interests you!
- Novels
- Newspapers
- Comic books
- Magazines

- Working crossword and other word puzzles. You will come across a variety of new words in a fun way.

Puzzle books range from easy to difficult. Answers are in the back.

- Reading "It Pays To Enrich Your Word Power." This is in each month's issue of *Reader's Digest*.

There is a 20-point quiz on one page with the answers on the next page.

- Studying the lists of prefixes, roots, and suffixes found in the appendix at the back of this book.

The different parts give you clues to the word's meaning.

E.

How can I get down on paper what I really want to say?

The most difficult part of approaching a writing assignment is getting your thoughts from your head to the paper in an organized fashion. Viewing writing as a process rather than as a one-shot operation can help. The writing process can be reduced to three steps:

1) brainstorming, which helps to generate ideas,
2) organizing, which involves combining those ideas in a logical way, and
3) revising, which means fine tuning your essay in regard to overall sense, sentence structure, grammar, and spelling.

The tips below are designed to help you with brainstorming, organizing, and revising your written work.

1. **Discuss what you want to say** with someone before you begin to write.

It will help you figure out what you want to write.

2. **Brainstorm ideas** about your topic and diagram them.

   A. Brainstorm by writing down every word that pops into your head about the topic.

   B. Group the words that go together.

   C. Choose a heading for each group.

   D. Write the words under their heading.

   E. Write a topic sentence. Use the words you chose for a heading.

accidents, snow plows, cold, shovels, sleet, windy, blowers, school closings

blizzard

cleaning up: shovels, snowplows, blowers

effects: accidents, school closings

weather: cold, windy, sleet

The blizzard's nasty weather kept most people inside.

3. Use the "unfinished story" technique:

A. Write a "starter sentence."

On the day of the storm, schools were closed.

B. "Brainstorm." Write down every word that pops into your head about the topic.

snow, ice skating, plows, danger, cold, sleet, snowmen

C. Use those words in sentences.

The snow and cold sleet made trying to drive very dangerous.

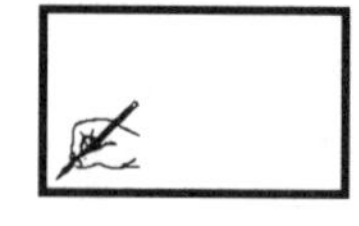

4. Practice writing by keeping a daily journal of your thoughts. Date your pages, so you can see your progress.

The more writing you do, the easier it will be.

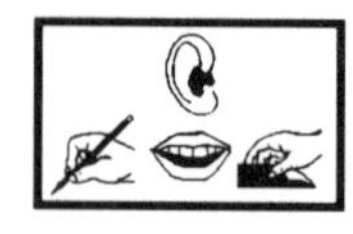

5. Use a tape recorder to dictate your letter or paper. Then play it back and write down what you have said.

It is easier for most people to talk about things than to write about them.

6. Have someone write down what you dictate. She will be able to question anything that isn't clearly stated.

A supervisor often dictates letters to her assistant.

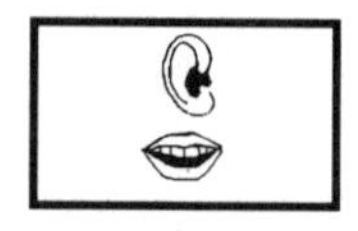

7. Have someone read what you have written out loud to you. Does it say what you wanted to say?

This will give you an idea of how it sounds to other people.

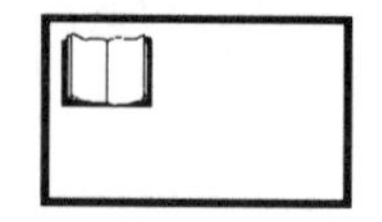

8. Read to someone what you have written. Ask that person to react to it. Use those reactions to guide your revisions.

9. Write and rewrite!

A. First draft: just keep writing without worrying about grammar, spelling, or punctuation. You will deal with these later.

Focus on getting your ideas down on paper.

B. Put your first draft aside for a day. You will be able to look at it more objectively if you get away from it for a while.

C. Second draft: time to revise.

- Reword things that don't sound right.
- Add new information.
- Rearrange the order of ideas.

Keep rewriting until it is the way you want it.

D. Put your second draft aside for a day.

E. Proofread your paper.

F. Write or type the final copy.

Read the "general tip" below for a proofreading hint.

General Tip: **When proofreading your own work,** it is easier to catch spelling errors by reading the paper backwards (starting at the end). You will be able to concentrate on each word individually, instead of reading the paper for content.

F.

How can I improve the appearance of my written work?

1. **Use good writing tools.**
   - Sharp pencil
   - Pencil that is a comfortable length
   - Pen that doesn't leave blobs of ink
   - Typewriter ribbons that make a dark copy

Good writing tools will improve the overall appearance of your work and will put you in the right frame of mind to do good work.

2. **Use a good writing position.**
   - Sit at a table or desk.
   - Write on a firm, solid surface.
   - Rest your arms comfortably on the desk or tabletop.

Compare the differences in your writing when you are writing in different locations and in different positions. Which looks best?

3. **Use an electronic typewriter.** Built-in sounds alert you to misspelled words. This lets you use words in your speaking vocabulary that you might be afraid to use in writing because you are unsure of the spelling.

Your larger vocabulary will make a better impression.

4. **Use a word-processing program.** There are many different programs to choose from. Word-processing programs let you:
   - Move information around without retyping the entire manuscript
   - Add or delete information quickly
   - Make speedy corrections
   - Make error-free copies in less time than it takes to handwrite them or type them on a typewriter

Word-processing programs save you time and produce professional-looking work.

CHAPTER 9

Mathematics

How do you react when you hear the word *mathematics?* Do you shrink away from the subject? Do you immediately think to yourself, "I'm no good at math"? Do you think of math as having no use in the real world?

If you answered "yes" to any of these questions, you're not alone. Many people respond negatively when faced with mathematics. There are things you can do, however, to approach math in a positive way.

One thing you can do is remember that math is a language. You need to "read" plus signs and minus signs to get mathematical meaning in much the same way you read a sentence to get meaning from words.

You can also approach math more positively once you recognize how often you need to use it in your everyday life. Estimating prices, making change, figuring tips, and calculating discounts are just a few ways you probably already use math every day.

Read through the following statements dealing with mathematics. Sit back and think about each statement. Be honest! This is a personal survey, so it can only help you if you are honest about yourself.

Put a check mark in front of the statements that describe you:

____ A. I confuse plus and minus signs when I add and subtract.

____ B. I cannot keep my numerals lined up on the paper.

____ C. I change the order of numerals when I copy them.

____ D. Number facts are hard for me to memorize.

____ E. I have trouble estimating.

____ F. Word problems give me trouble.

____ G. I don't know how much to tip.

____ H. I don't know how to figure out discounts in stores.

Choose the checked statement that is the most important to you at this time and note the letter to the right of your check mark. Turn to the section of this chapter that begins with that letter. Look for strategies that have the symbols for your preferred learning styles pictured in the left-hand column. Choose one of these strategies and follow the directions in the center column. Read the comments in the right-hand column for more hints. Try the strategy four or five times to see if it works for you. If it doesn't, try another. Strategies can be used individually or in combinations. Help yourself!

How can I stop confusing plus and minus signs?

General Tip: Think of the minus sign (-) as "pulling things away" from the other number, so the answer will be less.

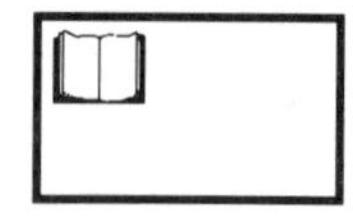

1. **Pay close attention** to the sign when you read the problem. Ask yourself, "What is this sign? Does it mean that I should add or subtract?"

Decide whether to add or subtract *before* you do the problem.

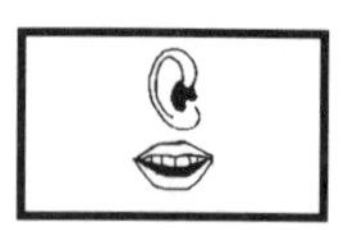

2. **Talk to yourself as you do the problem.**

This will help you think through the problem.

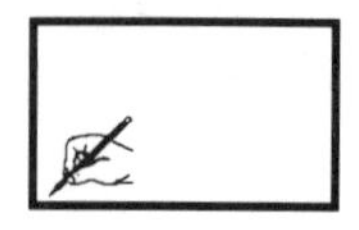

3. **Circle the sign before you begin work.** The circle will call attention to the sign, so you will focus more on which operation to use.

129 ⊖72   148 ⊕9

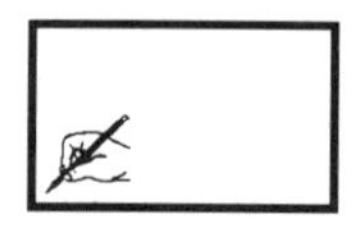

4. **Darken the plus and minus signs before you start working.** Darkening them will call attention to the differences between the signs.

129 −72   148 + 9

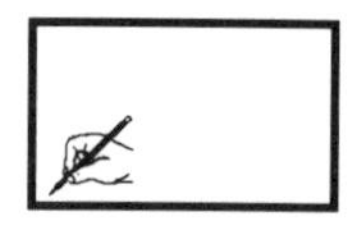

5. **Write the words "plus" and "minus" by the signs.** This will make you stop and think about what to do.

129 minus −72   148 plus + 9

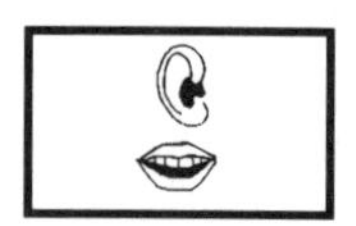

6. **Check with someone** who excels in math to be sure you are doing the problems correctly.

"Will you please help me? I sometimes mix up adding and subtracting."

B.

How can I keep my numerals lined up on the paper?

1. **As you write each digit,** give it room to be in its own column, so you work with the correct numerals.

Numerals must be lined up correctly to get the right answer.

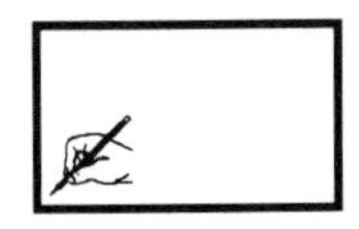

2. **Circle the number of the problem** to keep it separate from the problem itself.

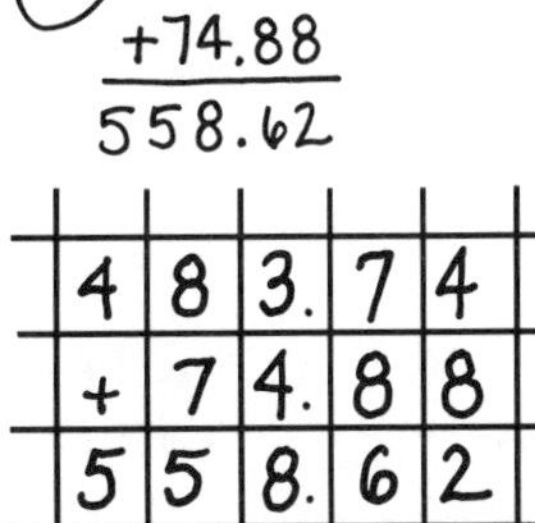

3. **Use graph paper to keep numerals lined up.** Allow one numeral per square.

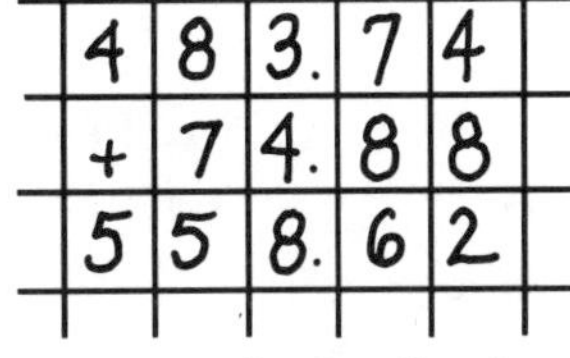

4. **Fold the paper into columns** to keep the numerals lined up.

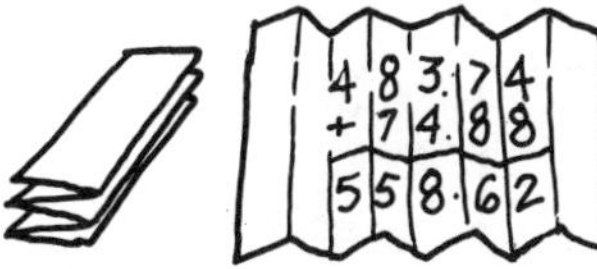

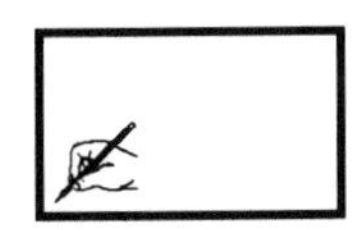

5. **Draw vertical lines on your paper.** Allow one numeral per column.

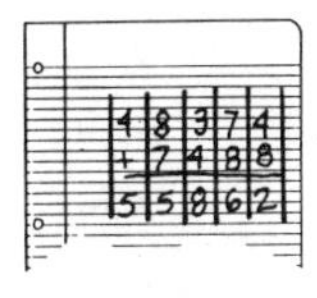

6. **Turn your narrow-lined paper sideways** to make columns to line up your numerals. Circle the number of the problem, so you don't think that it is part of the problem.

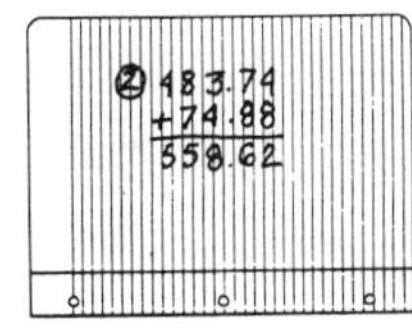

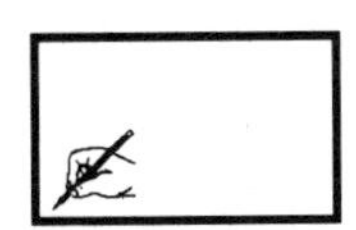

7. **Cover up all of the columns except the one you are working on.** Using a piece of paper or a ruler, keep moving it to the left, one column at a time, as you work the problem.

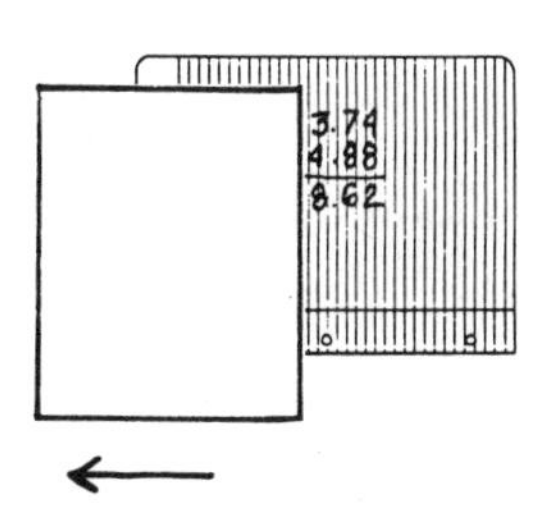

C.

What can I do if I write my numerals in a different order when I copy them on my paper?

Awareness is the key to this problem. If you are asking this question, you are halfway to solving it!

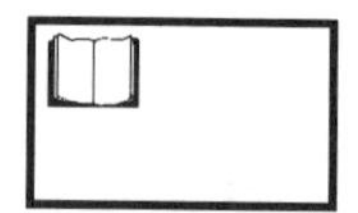

1. **Always proofread what you have written.** Compare it with the original before you start to work the problem.

Check to be sure you haven't written 49 for 94.

2. **Say the numerals out loud slowly as you write them.**

This will help you concentrate on the order.

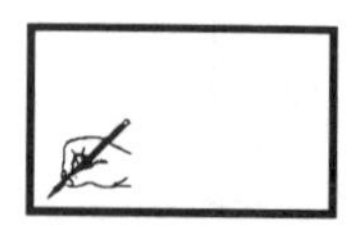

3. **Write the numerals slowly.**

When you write fast, you are apt to be careless.

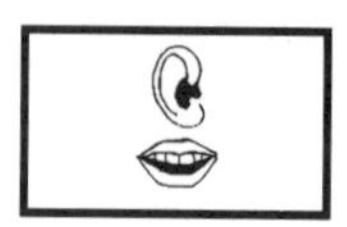

4. **Ask someone to read to you what you have written.** Listen to be sure that you wrote what you meant to write.

Pay close attention to each number you hear.

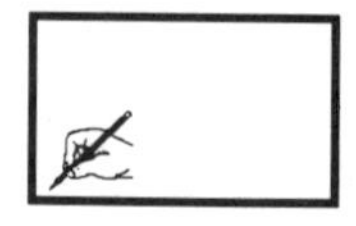

5. **Write down what you are doing or how you are feeling when the trouble happens.** Then be careful during those times.

- In a hurry?
- Tired?
- Watching TV?
- Talking?
- Thinking about something else?

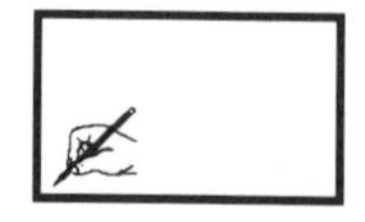

6. **Write out the words for the numerals** when you are giving a speech.

Instead of 459, write it out: four hundred fifty-nine.

D.

How can I memorize number facts?

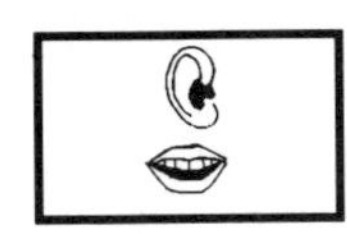

1. **Chant the numerals in a rhythm.** It will sound like a cheer at a sporting event.

5 plus 8 is 13
5 times 7 is 35

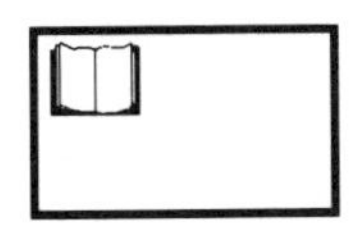

2. **Use correctly completed addition and multiplication tables.** Keep these tables in your study area to refer to as you do your work.

See the addition and multiplication tables on the next page.

3. **Make a stack of blank multiplication tables.** Keep them handy, so you can practice often! Always check your answers against the answers on your guide.

Request blank tables from your math teacher.

4. **Make flash cards of the facts.** Write the problem on the front and the answer on the back.

Front:	Back:
7 ×8	56

A. Read the problem side first.
Give the answer.

7 x 8 =

B. Check your answer with the answer side.

56

C. Separate the cards into two piles. As you test yourself, put the cards you answer correctly five times in the "I know" pile. Put the cards you answer incorrectly in the "Must study" pile. When all the cards are in the "I know" pile, review the whole pack again.

"Five times" means during five different practice sessions, not all in the same sitting!

D. Keep using the flash cards until you can answer them all correctly.

Say them out loud!
Write them! If you miss a card, it must go back into the "Must study" pile.

Addition Table

+	0	1	2	3	4	5	6	7	8	9
0	0	1	2	3	4	5	6	7	8	9
1	1	2	3	4	5	6	7	8	9	10
2	2	3	4	5	6	7	8	9	10	11
3	3	4	5	6	7	8	9	10	11	12
4	4	5	6	7	8	9	10	11	12	13
5	5	6	7	8	9	10	11	12	13	14
6	6	7	8	9	10	11	12	13	14	15
7	7	8	9	10	11	12	13	14	15	16
8	8	9	10	11	12	13	14	15	16	17
9	9	10	11	12	13	14	15	16	17	18

Multiplication Table

x	0	1	2	3	4	5	6	7	8	9
0	0	0	0	0	0	0	0	0	0	0
1	0	1	2	3	4	5	6	7	8	9
2	0	2	4	6	8	10	12	14	16	18
3	0	3	6	9	12	15	18	21	24	27
4	0	4	8	12	16	20	24	28	32	36
5	0	5	10	15	20	25	30	35	40	45
6	0	6	12	18	24	30	36	42	48	54
7	0	7	14	21	28	35	42	49	56	63
8	0	8	16	24	32	40	48	56	64	72
9	0	9	18	27	36	45	54	63	72	81

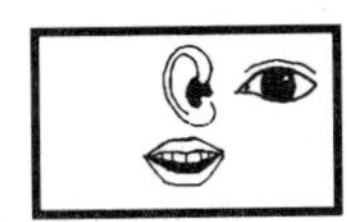

5. **Work from the number facts you already know** to reason out the answer you don't know.

"I don't know 6 x 9, but I know that 6 x 10 is 60. I can subtract 6 from 60 and get the answer of 54."

6. **Use a drill calculator to practice number facts.** This will help you learn number facts and speed up your recall of the facts. You can set the level of difficulty on these calculators.

You can buy a drill calculator in discount stores.

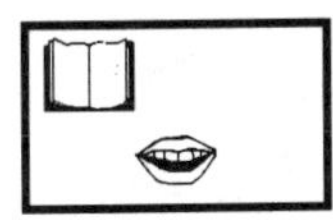

7. **Learn these aids for checking multiplication.**

- Answers to the 5s end in 0 or 5.

  5 x 2 = 1**0**　　5 x 5 = 2**5**

- Answers to the 10s end in 0.

  2 x 10 = 2**0**　　5 x 10 = 5**0**

- Answers to the 2s end in multiples of 2: 2, 4, 6, 8, 0.

  2 x 2 = **4**　　2 x 8 = 1**6**

- In every multiple of 9, the sum of the digits is 9.

  6 x 9 = **54** (**5** + **4** = **9**)
  7 x 9 = **63** (**6** + **3** = **9**)

E.

How can I estimate?

General Tip: When you estimate, round the original numbers to numbers that are easier to work with.

Round $.89 to $1.00 instead of $.90 to make your work easier.

1. **When estimating the cost of several items,** it is better to round up. This way, the bill won't be more than you expect.

Round $.89 to $1.00
Round $1.39 to $1.50
Round $2.29 to $2.50

2. **Carry a small notebook and use it to write down your estimates** if you are estimating many items.

curling iron	$15.00
toothpaste	$ 2.00
deodorant	$ 2.50
2 greeting cards	$ 3.00
Soda	$ 3.00
	$ 25.50

3. **Carry a calculator with you.**

Pocket calculators are inexpensive and durable.

F.

How can I do word problems more easily?

Thinking through word problems before you try to do them will make your job easier. The tips below will help you.

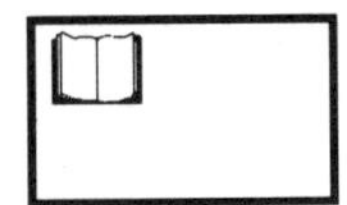

1. Read the entire problem twice before you try to work it out. If you have trouble understanding the problem, read it again.

This will help you to understand how the pieces of information are related.

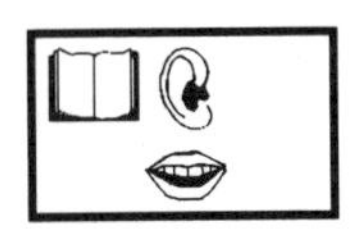

2. Read the entire problem out loud to yourself.

You may read more slowly and carefully out loud.

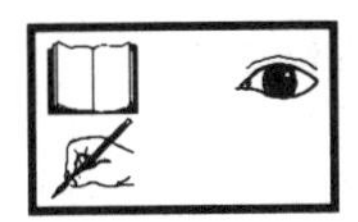

3. Draw a picture or diagram of the problem whenever possible.

Example: "Tori ran 6 miles. Jenny ran 2 miles. Lisa ran 4 miles. How much farther did Tori run than Lisa?"

Tori: 6 miles
Jenny: 2 miles
Lisa: 4 miles

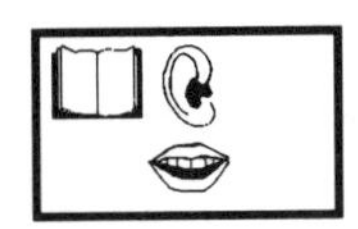

4. Talk to yourself about the problem.

Example: "Tori ran 6 miles. Jenny ran 2 miles. Lisa ran 4 miles. How much farther did Tori run than Lisa?"

"I only need to look at Tori and Lisa."

5. Cross out lightly the information you don't need to solve the problem.

In the example in number 4 above, you could cross out: ~~"Jenny ran 2 miles."~~

6. Circle all of the remaining numerals and their units. This will focus your attention on the information you will be working with.

In the example in number 4 above, you could circle: 6 miles and 4 miles.

7. Underline the question. Your answer must include the units the question is asking for (gallons, miles).

In the example in Tip 4 above, you could underline: "How much farther did Tori run than Lisa?"

8. **Reword the question.** This may help you to figure out what math operations are needed.

   Example: How much farther did Tori run than Lisa?

How many more miles did Tori run than Lisa?

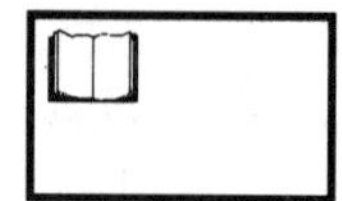

9. **Decide what math operations (+, -, x, ÷) are needed to solve the problem.** Focus on key words to help you decide which operations to use.

For example, *total, sum,* and *altogether* suggest addition.

10. **Estimate your answer by** rounding the given numbers to units that are easier to work with. Then do the problem and compare your answer with your estimate.

    Example: Charles wanted to buy a CD player that costs $199.95. He had saved $72.00. How much more did he need?

A. Round $199.95 to $200.
B. Round $72.00 to $70.
C. $200 - $70 = $130 (estimate)
D. $199.95 -$72.00 = $127.95 (answer)

General Tip: **Below is a five-step process you may find helpful in solving word problems.**

A. Read the problem and decide what information you need to use.

Cross out what you don't need.

B. Decide what math operations are needed to solve the problem.

C. Estimate your answer.

D. Do the problem and label the answer.

E. Check your answer.

Did you answer the question?
Is your answer close to your estimate?
Check the accuracy of your math operations.

G.

How can I figure out how much to tip?

Tips in restaurants are usually from 15% to 20%. Tips for other services range from 10% to 20%.

1. **Buy a tip card** in a stationery or book store. This card has a chart that tells you how much tip to leave.

These cards are the size of credit cards and fit easily into your wallet.

2. **Carry a calculator** and use it to figure the tip.

If your bill is $18.57, enter this amount. Push the x key, and punch 15 and the % key. Your answer will be $2.79. Round to $2.80 or $3.00.

3. **Double the amount of the tax to figure the tip** if your bill includes a food tax in the 7-10% range.

If the tax is 7%, leave a little more. If the tax is 10%, leave a little less.

4. **Figure out a 15% tip** using these three steps.

   A. Take 10% of the bill by moving the decimal one place to the left.

   10% of $13.14 is $1.31.

   B. Divide that number in half. Round the new number.

   1/2 of $1.31 is $.635. Round to $.65 or $.70.

   C. Add the answers from A and B to find the tip.

   $1.31 + $.65 = $1.96. Round to $2.00.

   Note: To figure a 20% tip, do step A and multiply by 2.

   $1.31 x 2 = $2.62. Round to $2.60.

H.

How can I figure out discounts?

Many stores have sales. Sometimes the merchandise is marked down with the new price shown on the price tag. Other times, the merchandise display is marked a certain percentage off, but the new price is not shown. The strategies below will help you figure out the new price when the merchandise is marked a certain percentage off.

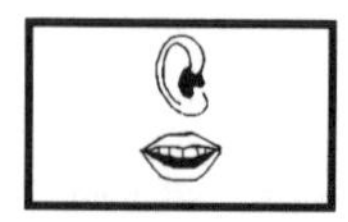

1. Ask a sales clerk for help.

This is the easiest way.

2. Use a calculator.

Suppose $24.99 jeans are discounted 15%.

A. Enter the regular price. — Enter $24.99.

B. Push the multiplication key. — Enter x.

C. Punch in the percentage off. — Enter 15% = $3.75

D. Subtract the answer in C from the regular price. Your answer is the discounted price. — $24.99 - $3.75 = $21.24

CHAPTER 10

Test Taking

Worry jams the channels of the brain just as static interferes with the picture on the TV screen. If you are going to show what you know on a test, you must get rid of that static. You need a clear channel to recall the information you have learned.

The strategies in this chapter will help you become test-wise in reading and taking tests. Think of test taking as a chance to show the teacher what you know. Start taking tests with the positive feeling that you have prepared for them in the best possible way.

Read through the following statements about test-taking anxiety and test-taking skills. Sit back and think about each statement. Be honest! This is a personal survey, so it can only help you if you are honest about yourself.

Put a check mark in front of the statements that describe you:

____ A. I don't know how to get organized before I study.

____ B. I don't know how to organize myself while I study.

____ C. I don't know how to score higher on tests.

____ D. I get really nervous right before a test.

____ E. When I take a test, I sometimes draw a blank.

____ F. I have trouble reading tests.

____ G. I usually don't have enough time to finish tests.

____ H. I have problems with multiple-choice tests.

____ I. I always do poorly on true/false tests.

____ J. I do not do well on essay tests.

Choose the checked statement that is the most important to you at this time and note the letter to the right of your check mark. Turn to the section of this chapter that begins with that letter. Look for strategies that have the symbols for your preferred learning styles pictured in the left-hand column. Choose one of these strategies and follow the directions in the center column. Read the comments in the right-hand column for more hints. Try the strategy four or five times to see if it works for you. If it doesn't, try another. Strategies can be used individually or in combinations. Help yourself!

How can I get organized before I study?

General Tip: **Make a checklist of things you need to know about every test.** Keep the list on the inside cover of each notebook.

Ask the teachers for this information. Be in the know—it's your right!

- The importance of the test

  How much will it count in your overall grade?

- What kind of test will it be?
  - True/false
  - Multiple-choice
  - Fill-in-the-blank
  - Essay
  - Open-book

  This will determine the way you study. Read Question B, Tip 2, in this chapter.

- Where will the questions come from?
  - Notes
  - Films
  - Handouts
  - Textbook
  - Speakers

  Are you missing notes on any of these?

- Are old tests available for review?

  Sample tests may be on file in the library.

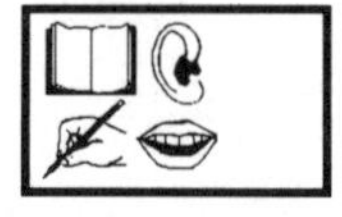

1. Make an appointment with the teacher before a major test.

A. Before the meeting, mark your notes.
- Circle things you don't understand.
- Write any questions you have in the margin.

Use a different color ink, so you can spot things easily during the conference.

B. During the meeting:
- Ask any questions that haven't been answered from your checklist for tests.

  Where will questions come from?
- Discuss any problems you're having taking her tests.

  Reading the tests? Finishing them in the allotted time?
- Discuss any special accommodations you need.

  More time?
  A different location?
  Someone to read it to you?

2. Check your inner and outer environments.

A. Inner environment (how you feel):
- Sleepy? — Get more sleep!
- Nervous? — Exercise.
- Unprepared? — Schedule more study time.

B. Outer environment (your study area):
- Poor light? — Add more light.
- Cold? — Add clothing, turn up heat.
- Missing supplies? — Gather them before studying.

3. Set goal dates as soon as you hear a test is scheduled.

Write the goals on the calendar in your study area. Check it before you start studying.

Example: You have five days before a test.

A. **Day 1**: Make a study guide. List facts, concepts, vocabulary.

See Chapter 7: Question G, Tip 4, Study guides.

B. **Day 2**: Test yourself on the study guide.

Study it until you know it.

C. **Day 3**: Reread the introduction, summary, headings, subheadings, and captions.

You are reviewing the main information for the test.

D. **Day 4**: Test yourself on section questions and chapter questions.

Look up the answers to the ones you don't know.

E. **Day 5**: Review your study guide and questions.

If you study every night, you won't have to cram the night before the test.

4. Fill in your lecture notes with any information you have missed.

Lecture notes are a major source of test questions.

A. Use the notes of an "A" student. This way you'll get complete notes.

If you're not sure whom to ask, discuss it with the teacher.

B. If possible, use the notes while the person is still in the room.

You can ask her questions!

5. **Plan how much time you'll study.** Write your time schedule down. Keep referring back to it, so you have enough time to study for each test.

   The night before the test should be spent reviewing, not learning the information for the first time.

   Example: You have three tests: one in science, one in English, and one in Spanish.

   - You have an "A" in science, so don't spend much time on it.

     Science
     30 min.
     6:30-7:00

   - You have strong English skills, so you will be able to study fairly quickly.

     English
     45 min.
     7:15-8:00

   - Your grade is down in Spanish, so you need to spend most of your time on this subject.

     Spanish
     1 hr. 30 min.
     8:30-10:00

B.

How can I organize myself while studying?

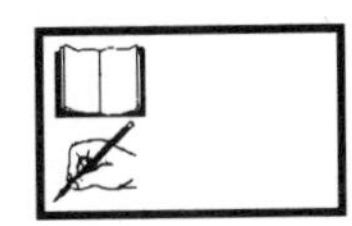

1. Make an informal outline.

A. List the headings from your textbook, lecture notes, and study guides.

Study time will then be focused on what's important.

B. Write words and phrases under these headings. Know what they mean and why they are important.

This is excellent essay test preparation.

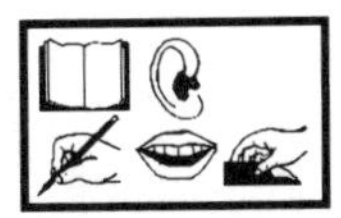

2. Study the way you will be tested.

Match the way you study to the type of test.

- Short-answer tests

  Write the answers while you are studying.

- Oral tests

  Say the information out loud.

- Matching and true/false tests

  Read the information over and over again, so it will "sound right" when you see it on the test.

- Essay tests

  Try to predict the essay questions you think will be on the test and answer them in writing.

- Open-book tests

  Know where the information is located in the book.

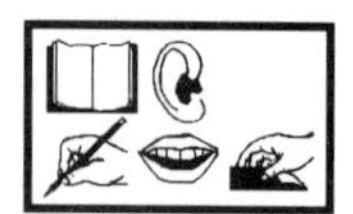

3. Make flash cards. Shuffle them often, so you don't learn the information in only one order.

Use index cards or cut up pieces of paper.

A. Write the question (term, date, fact) on one side, the answer on the other.

Read more information on flash cards in Chapter 4: Question E.

B. Make two piles of cards. As you test yourself, put the cards you answer correctly five times in the "I know" pile. Put the cards you answer incorrectly in the "Must study" pile. When all the cards are in the "I know" pile, review the whole pack again.

If you miss one card, it goes back into the "Must study" pile until you can answer it correctly in five different study sessions.

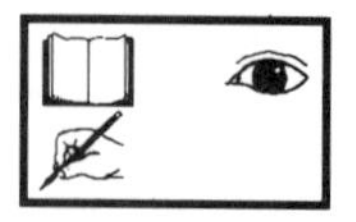

4. Diagram the information. Practice closing your eyes and "seeing" the diagram. During the test you will be able to give the correct answer because you will be able to "see" it.

Succession to the Presidency

President
Vice President
Speaker of the House
President Pro Tempore of Senate

5. Use a tape recorder to study for tests.

A. Record your review on tape.

1. Read the question. Count to five silently.

"When was the Civil War?"
1-2-3-4-5

2. Read the answer. Count to five silently before reading another question.

"1861-1865"
1-2-3-4-5

B. Answer the questions in writing.

1. Listen to the question. Push "pause."

2. Write the answer as you say it out loud. Let up "pause."

3. Listen to the answer. Check it against the one you have written.

If you gave the wrong answer, cross it out and write down the correct one.

C.

What can I do to score higher on tests?

General Tip: **Make use of any tutoring or support services** at your school. Discuss your needs with your advisor or counselor.

The decision to use these services is up to *you*, so you need to make your needs known.

1. **Prepare your mind and body.** It's easier to remember information if you are mentally and physically healthy.

Get enough sleep and eat a well-balanced diet.

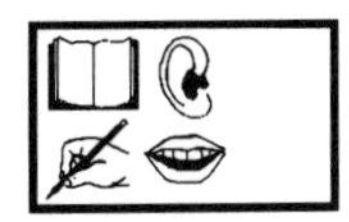

2. **Make an appointment with the teacher before and after the test.**

Write the teacher's office location and hours inside the cover of the appropriate notebook.

A. Before the test, discuss any questions about the test.

- Where will she get the questions? — Notes? Films? Handouts?
- What kind of test will it be? — Essay? T/F? Open book?
- Can you have extra time to finish? — "I have a reading problem."

B. After the test, discuss why you lost points.

Read the comments she wrote on your test paper for clues to what she's looking for.

- Incomplete study notes?
- Didn't study the right material?
- Didn't write enough on essays?

Find out where you made your mistakes and your grade will go up the next time.

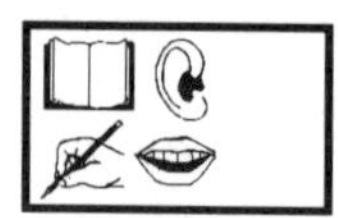

3. Don't miss review day!

Usually the day before the test.

A. Mark in your notebook the things she emphasizes.

Star these or write "impt." next to them.

B. Ask questions if you don't understand something.

Tomorrow will be too late.

C. Find out what kind of test it will be. This makes a difference in how you will study.

Read Question B, Tip 2, in this chapter.

- True/false?
- Multiple-choice?
- Fill-in-the-blank?
- Essay?
- Open-book?

D. Fill in any missing notes. Get them from an "A" student, so you are sure they will be complete.

If you are not sure whom to ask, check with the teacher.

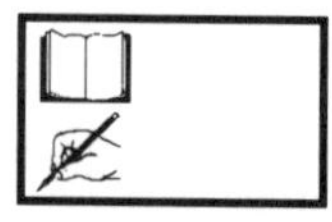

4. Skim your test paper as soon as you get it. Make sure you understand what you're supposed to do.

A. Write your name or initials on each page, so they don't get lost.

B. Read the directions for each section.

1. Mark the key words in the directions.
2. Number the things you're asked to do.

Circle the verb and correct the punctuation.

1 Circle the verb and
2 correct the punctuation.

D.

How can I calm down right before a test?

A little nervousness is good for you. It keeps you alert. But too much anxiety can prevent you from doing well on a test. Try these relaxation exercises if you're too nervous before a test.

1. **Take deep breaths.**

   A. Stare at the desk, wall, or floor and take a breath so deep it seems to pull the air from the bottom of your feet.

   Don't make any noise or pump your shoulders up and down.

   B. When you can't take in any more air, hold your breath for a count of five. Then let the air out slowly through your nose.

   Try to visualize the air as it travels through your body and out through your nose.

   C. Repeat five times.

2. **Push your feet down** on the floor to a slow count of five. Push them down harder and harder. Relax. Do it again.

   Do this five times. This will take your mind off the test.

3. **Walk around** if you are allowed to do so; get a drink, sharpen your pencil, take a trip to the bathroom, or look out the window.

   Exercise will help relax you and will allow you to think about other things.

4. **Shake your arms** down by your sides as you take deep breaths.

   You will shake loose some body tension.

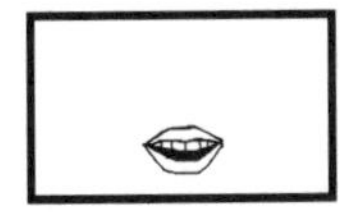

5. **"Psyche" yourself** into doing well by saying positive things to yourself.

   "I've studied hard, and I'm going to do well on this."

6. **Visualize.** Close your eyes and think about a place where you feel happy and peaceful. Visualize yourself in this place. "See" how it looks, "feel" the wind and sun, "smell" the flowers.

Open your eyes and notice how relaxed you've become!

General Tip: **Be realistic** about your situation. If you haven't studied enough, tell yourself that you still have to take this test and that you'll give it your best effort.

Study properly for the next test.

E.

What can I do when I blank out during a test?

If you "blank out" during a test, it means you cannot remember what you have studied. Your mind is a "blank." It is usually a result of being too nervous. You must calm yourself down so you can think clearly again.

1. **Use relaxation techniques.**
   - Take deep breaths without making any noise. Fill your lungs, and hold your breath for a count of five. Let the air out slowly through your nose.

     Deep breaths put more oxygen into the brain.

   - Shake your arms down by your sides.

     Loosen up body tension.

   - Count slowly to 25 while staring at the floor, desk, or wall.

     This takes your mind off the test.

2. **Change your test-taking location.** Discuss your anxiety problem with the teacher. Alternative locations might be the library, office, conference room, or counselor's office.

   Peer pressure often makes a person very nervous and can be a cause of going "blank."

3. **"Brainstorm."** In the margin or on the back of the paper, write as many words as you can think of about the topic. Don't stop to decide if a word is important or spelled correctly. Just keep your pen moving without stopping.

   Writing words helps to unlock your memory, so you will be able to remember the material you studied.

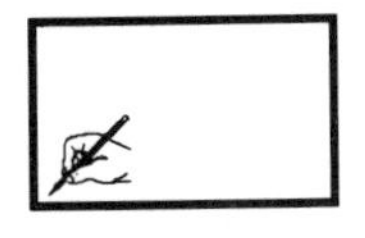

4. **Move on to the next question** if you don't know an answer. Circle the number of the one you didn't answer, so you can come back to it later.

   Don't get stuck on one question. The answer may be found in another section.

5. **Fold the test paper,** so you can only see the section you are working on.

   Looking at the entire test can make a person panic.

F.

What can I do if I have trouble reading tests?

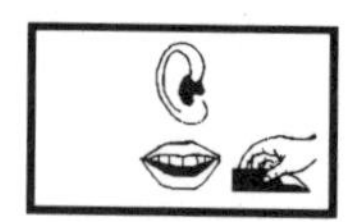

1. **Discuss your reading problem** with the teacher. Arrangements can be made to have someone read the test to you, allow you more time, or seat you in a different room where someone can answer questions for you. That person can:

   It is important that *you* take the initiative to explain your reading problem and ask for modifications to be made.

   - Eliminate errors due to your mistaking one word for another word.

     "crate" for "cremate"

   - Reword a question, so it may be easier for you to understand.

     Change "Explain the family's economic structure" to "How did they budget their money?"

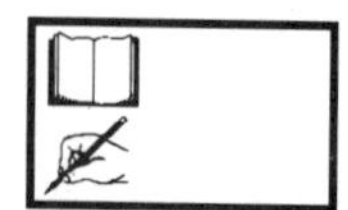

2. **Answer only the questions you are sure of first.** As you read through the test, you may find answers to the ones you weren't sure of.

   Knowing these answers will give you more confidence and speed you·up.

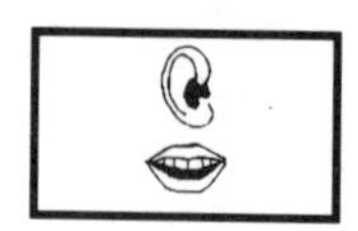

3. **Ask the teacher what a question means.** After she has explained it to you, repeat it to her in your own words to be sure you have understood the question.

   "What does this mean?"

   "What you want to know is ..."

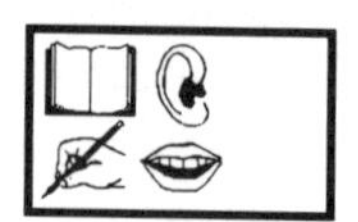

4. **Circle words you can't pronounce or don't know the meaning of.**

   Try these strategies:
   - Skim the test looking for the circled word in another part of the test.

     The way it is used in a different sentence may help you understand it.

   - Skip the circled word and read the rest of the sentence. Then go back and guess at what it means by the words that come before and after it.

     This is called using "context clues."

   - Ask the teacher for help.

     This is the fastest way.

5. Keep working on the test until your time is up. Proofread your test if you have any time left over.

Don't feel pressured by students who have turned in their tests early.

G.

What can I do if I don't finish tests on time?

You must figure out why you aren't finishing tests on time. Do any of the questions below describe you? If yes, try the strategies under that question the next time you take a test.

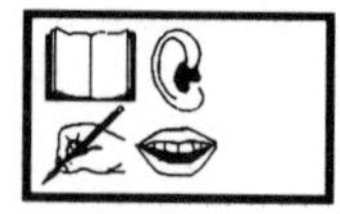

1. Do you have trouble understanding the words?

- Skim the test looking for those words in another place on the test.

  Seeing other ways they are used may help you.

- Skip the word you don't know and read the rest of the sentence. Then go back and guess what the word means by the words that come before and after it.

  This is called using "context clues."

- Ask the teacher what the word means.

  This is the fastest way.

- Discuss your reading problem with the teacher.

  She can get you help or give you extra time.

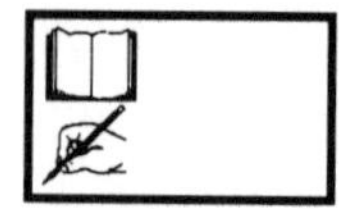

2. Do you take too much time on individual questions?

- Write a time limit by each section. Spend more time on sections that are worth more points.

  Section 1 (20 pts.): 10 min.
  Section 2 (40 pts.): 20 min.

- Answer only the questions you're sure of the first time you go through the test. Do this as quickly as you can.

  Then judge how much time you have left to work on the ones you don't know.

- Take a guess if time is running out.

  Guess only as a last resort.

3. Do you daydream and lose your concentration?

- Ask the teacher if you can take the test in another room.

  Get away from peer pressure and distractions.

- Try to stay within your time limits.

  Keep checking the clock!

- Get enough rest, so you aren't tired.

  Being tired makes it harder to concentrate.

4. Do you get nervous and panic?

- Take deep breaths. Hold a breath for a count of five. Let the air out slowly through your nose.

  Do this five times.

- Take the test in another room.

  Prearrange this.

- Get the voice inside your head going.

  "I've studied hard and I'm going to do well on this test."

How can I do better on multiple-choice tests?

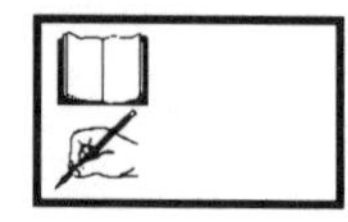

1. **Circle key words in the directions.** Do this before you start taking the test. This will help you be clear on what you are supposed to do.

"Write the letter of the answer"
"Circle the best answer..."

2. **Follow this two-step process.**

   A. Read through all of the questions.

   First reading

      1. Answer only the ones you are sure of.

      2. Circle the numerals of the ones you aren't sure of. Come back to them later.

      3. Look for answers to the ones you don't know as you read through the rest of the test.

      You may find the answer within another question.

   B. For questions that you're still having trouble with, try the following:

   Second reading

      1. Underline key words as you read through the question again.

      These words will change the meaning of a sentence.

      never always less
      not only more all

      2. Read the question and cross out all of the answers you know are wrong.

      This is called the "process of elimination."

      3. Reread the question with each of the remaining answers to see which answer sounds right.

      Your first instinct will usually be right.

General Tip: **Answer every question.** Guess only when you have to.

Your brain may "kick out" the right answer without your realizing it.

I.

How can I do better on true/false tests?

General Tip: **Don't think of true/false tests as "sneaky"** or filled with "trick" questions. You'll read things into them that aren't there. And remember, always answer every question. You have a 50-50 chance of being right.

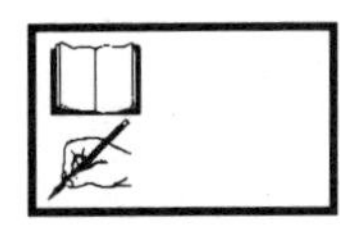

1. **Circle key words in the directions.** What are you supposed to write?

"True" and "False"?
"T" and "F"?
"+" and "-"?

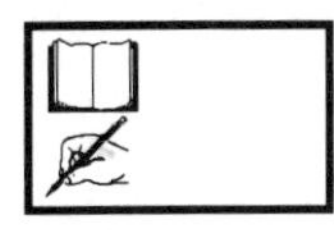

2. **Do the ones you are sure of first.** Circle the numerals of the ones you aren't sure of, so you will remember to go back and do them.

Look for answers to the ones you don't know while you read through the rest of the test.

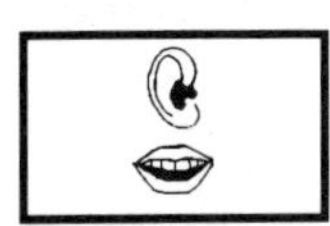

3. **Read the ones you aren't sure of out loud** (or under your breath).

They might make more sense when you hear them.

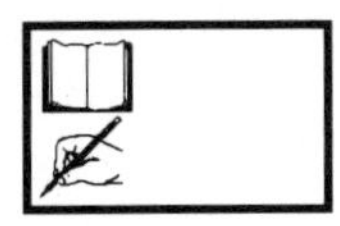

4. **If a question has a double negative** in it, cross out both negatives.

Change "It is not unreasonable to expect Americans to vote" to "It is reasonable to expect Americans to vote."

5. Guess as a last resort.

A. Statements are usually **false** when these "absolute" words are found in the statement.

everyone	nobody	only
all	always	none
never	no one	

"All Americans eat hamburgers."

B. Statements are usually **true** when:

- These qualifying words are found in the statement:

generally	probably	some
frequently	sometimes	most
usually	seldom	maybe
often		

"Frequently made trips to the shopping mall cost a lot of money."

- It is a "teacher-made" test and there are no "absolute" words in the statement.

- They are long and involved.

"Teaching interventions occur when a student doesn't reach mastery."

J.

How can I do better on essay tests?

General Tip: **Pretend the person reading the essay doesn't know anything about the topic.** That way, you'll always be able to write something.

1. **Estimate the time** you think it will take you to complete the essay. The more points, the more time you will need. Write down the time you should start the essay under your estimated time. Keep track of your time.

You will need to write more for a 50-point essay than a 20-point one.

Essay 1: 10 min.
9:00 - 9:10

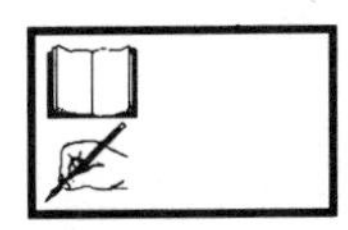

2. **Circle the key words in the directions.** These words tell you what to do.

Explain and give examples of the reasons students drop out of school.

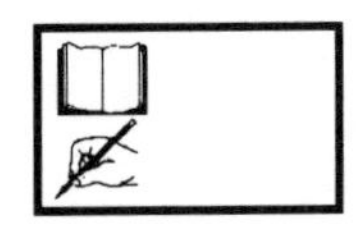

3. **Number each thing you're asked to do.**

1. Explain and 2. give examples of the reasons students drop out of school.

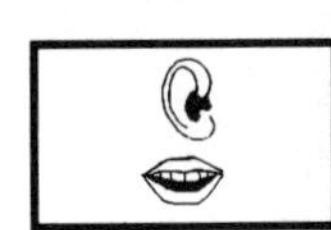

4. **Put the directions into your own words.** This will help you stick to the subject and give only the information you're asked for.

"I need to write about why kids drop out of school."

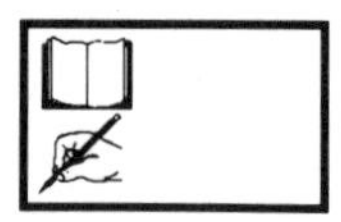

5. **Brainstorm for one minute** before you start writing the essay.

   A. Write down all of the words that pop into your head about the topic. Keep your pen moving without stopping!

   need full-time job
   failing classes
   bored by school
   want to move out
   want to get married
   reading problems

   B. Group the words that go together.

   failing classes
   bored by school
   reading problems

   need full-time job
   want to move out
   want to get married

   C. Label the groups in the order you want to use them in the essay.

   Personal Reasons
   need full-time job
   want to move out.
   want to get married

   Educational Reasons
   failing classes
   bored by school
   reading problems

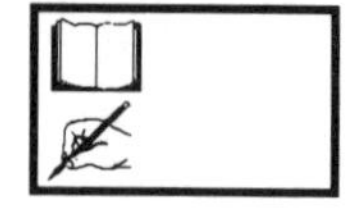

6. **Make sure your essay has these three main parts:**

   A. Topic sentence/introduction: Reword the directions to form a topic sentence.

   Dropping out of school has personal and educational causes.

   B. Body: Explain in detail the key concepts you listed. (Read Question J, Tip 5 in this chapter.)

   One personal reason is needing a full-time job...

   C. Conclusion: Reword your topic sentence and add a few supporting details.

   Students do not finish school for many reasons. Some may be personal, like needing a full-time job. Others may be educational, like failing grades. These are just some reasons for today's high dropout rate.

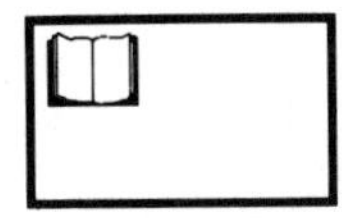

7. **Proofread your essay before handing it in.** Is your essay:
   - Easy to read?
   - In paragraph form?
   - In proper grammatical form?
   - Punctuated correctly?
   - Free of spelling errors?

Read your essay out loud (or under your breath) to pick up punctuation errors, run-on sentences, and sentence fragments.

Appendix

Helpful Word Lists

A. Short Vowels

a—*hand*
apathy
antisocial
apprehension
advantageous

e—*neck*
education
embarking
leggings
impenetrable

i—*lips*
fixation
wickedness
discontinuation
permission

o—*body*
oxbow
ophthalmology
dislodge
illogical

u—*thumb*
bankrupt
presumptuous
plunder
bunions

y—*crystal*
dyslexia
paralysis
symphony
synthetic

B. Long Vowels

Long A

ai—*rain*
ailment
unassailable
restraint
acquaintance

a_e—*game*
validate
hydroplane
lemonade
cascade

ei—*freight*
reindeer
surveillance
beige
unfeigned

ey—*survey*
conveyor
preying
abeyance
greyhound

ay—*day*
defraying
mayonnaise
bayonet
prepayment

ea—*steak*
break
greatly
outbreak
Great Plains

eigh—*eight*
neighbors
sleigh
weightless
freight

Long E

ea—*beach*
interweave
upheaval
weakening
tweak

e_e *delete*
centipede
indiscrete
recede
athlete

ey—*key*
trolley
hockey
attorney
abbey

y—*trophy*
transparency
serenity
tyranny
ability

ee—*sleep*
pedigree
Tennessee
discreet
tureen

ei—*receive*
conceited
codeine
receipt
Neil

ie—*piece*
thievery
yielding
diesel
eerie

i_e—*magazine*
gasoline
figurine
vaccine
routine

Long I

i_e—*five*
connive
neutralize
serialize
editorialize

igh—*night*
rightfully
foresight
nightingale
twilight

y—*my*
dying
typhoon
carbohydrate
specify

y_e—*thyme*
analyze
formaldehyde
prototype
paralyze

Long O

eau—*beau*
plateau
trousseau
chateau
Trudeau

oa—*soap*
reproach
bloated
goatee
cocoa

oe—*toe*
oboe
woe
Ivanhoe
aloe

o_e—*stone*
compote
envelope
revoke
stovepipe

olk—*folk*
folklore
polka
polka dot
yolk

ost—*post*
mostly
ghost
postpone
guidepost

ou—*dough*
although
thorough
borough
furlough

oul—*soul*
boulder
shoulder
poultry
soulful

ow—*sparrow*
Owen
wallow
escrow
tomorrow

Long U

ew—*new*
mildew
shrewdness
renew
Andrew

ew—*view*
askew
curfew
nephew
ewe

o—*ado*
approval
improve
movement
remover

oo—*bamboo*
shampoo
foolproof
loosen
soothing

ou—*group*
coupon
routine
youthful
soup

u—*menu*
rumor
human
unionize
universe

ue—*cue*
residue
Tuesday
discontinue
argue

ue—*blue*
gruesome
glue
clues
sue

u_e—*fume*
immune
computer
rebuke
molecule

C. Other Vowel Sounds

ar—*parent*
variation
transparent
hilarious
vegetarian

arr—*carry*
marriage
barren
embarrass
arrogant

au—*August*
nautical
applause
astronaut
laundry

aw—*jaw*
lawyer
awesome
rickshaw
awning

ear—*ear*
clear
spear
yearling
smearing

ear—*heard*
search
earnest
yearning
research

ear—*bear*
overbearing
wearing
forbear
tear

er—*very*
verify
therapy
geriatric
sterilize

er—*river*
whimpering
interpret
termite
terminology

er—*zero*
cereal
mysterious
bacteria
deteriorate

err—*error*
territory
serrated
terrace
herring

ia—*media*
cafeteria
bacteria
criteria
Australia

ia—*trial*
denial
liability
viable
diagram

ir—*first*
Virginia
circumvent
squirting
infirmary

oi—*oil*
appointment
poinsettia
anoint
boisterous

oo—*took*
crooked
understood
afoot
neighborhood

or—*born*
forlorn
davenport
scorch
orthopedics

ou—*soup*
Louis
route
rouge
group

ou—*found*
ouch
pronounce
astound
trousers

ough—*thought*
bought
nought
overwrought
forethought

ow—*brown*
rowdy
allowable
scowl
howitzer

oy—*joy*
annoyance
gargoyle
flamboyant
clairvoyant

ur—*turn*
disturbance
undercurrent
lurkingly
surgery

ure—*future*
maturity
procedure
obscure
secure

our—*your*
contour
tourist
detour
courier

D. Silent Consonants

bt—*debt*
doubtful
subtlety
indebted
debtor

ck—*black*
sprocket
recklessness
ransack
quickly

gh—*ghost*
Afghanistan
aghast
ghetto
ghastly

ght—*light*
thought
straight
weight
frightened

gn—*gnome*
gnat
gnarled
cologne
campaign

kn—*knee*
knightly
knucklebone
Knoxville
acknowledge

lk—*walk*
chalk
folklore
polka
balk

lm—*calm*
palmistry
balmy
embalmment
psalm

rh—*rhino*
rhythmic
rhinestone
rhododendron
rheumatism

mb—*lamb*
plumbers
tombstone
combing
thumbnail

mn—*condemn*
columns
condemning
autumn
solemnly

sc—*science*
scenery
descend
transcendentalism
scintillating

stle—*wrestle*
thistle
epistle
hustle
whistling

wr—*wrist*
wrenchingly
playwright
wrangling
wreath

E. Prefixes

ab *(away from)*
abnormal
absenteeism
absorption
abstinence

ad *(toward)*
admittedly
advertisement
advisable
adhesive

ambi *(both)*
ambidextrous
ambivalent
ambiguity
ambiguous

ante *(before)*
antemortem
anteroom
antecedent
antebellum

anti *(against)*
antislavery
antitrust
antisocial
antibiotic

arch *(main)*
archetype
archbishop
archangel
archrival

auto *(self)*
autograph
autobiography
automatic
autonomous

be *(intensive)*
belabor
bedazzlement
begrudge
bemused

bene *(good)*
benefits
benediction
benevolence
benefactor

bi *(two)*
biceps
binoculars
bilingual
bicycle

cent *(100)*
century
centennial
centimeter
centenarian

circum *(around)*
circumvent
circumspect
circumference
circumstantial

com *(together)*
combustible
composition
compatible
companion

contra *(against)*
contrary
contradiction
contrasting
contraindicate

de *(undoing)*
delocalize
deactivate
detraction
decentralization

di *(two, double)*
dichloride
dichotomy
diatribe
dilemma

dis *(apart)*
disharmony
disarmament
disconcerted
disenchantment

en *(into)*
enthrone
encompass
encouragement
endangered

epi *(close to, on)*
epicenter
epicycle
epidemic
epidermis

ex *(out)*
excavation
execute
exceptional
expulsion

fore *(front)*
forebode
forecast
foreclose
foreground

hydro *(water)*
hydroelectric
hydrodynamically
hydroplane
hydropower

hyper *(great)*
hypertechnical
hyperexcited
hyperconscientious
hypersensitive

in *(not)*
inactive
inaccessible
inattentive
incalculable

inter *(among)*
interchange
interruption
interfere
intermediary

intro *(into)*
introduction
intromission
introvert
introspection

macro *(large, great)*
macrocosm
macrostructure
macroclimatology
macroeconomics

mal *(bad)*
malevolent
malicious
malignant
maladjusted

micro *(small)*
microscopic
microanalysis
microbe
microelectronics

mis *(wrong)*
misbehave
misdeed
misapprehension
misorientation

mono *(one)*
monogram
monosyllable
monotonous
monochromatic

multi *(many)*
multifold
multinational
multicolored
multiplication

non *(not)*
nonconductor
nonconformist
nondenominational
nonsense

omni *(all)*
omniscient
omnivore
omnipotent
omnibus

per *(thoroughly)*
perfume
perchance
perfection
perennial

poly *(many)*
polygraph
polygamy
polysyllabic
polygon

post *(after)*
postponement
postgraduate
postscript
postoperative

pre *(before)*
preschool
precaution
predetermine
preparedness

pro *(support)*
production
proclaim
prorevolutionary
processional

re *(again)*
rebate
rebound
reassurance
repetitive

retro *(back)*
retrograde
retroaction
retrogress
retrospectively

sub *(under)*
submarine
subway
subdivision
subterranean

super *(above)*
superachiever
superintendent
superabundant
superimpose

syn *(together)*
synthesize
synergistic
synchronize
syndicated

tele *(distance)*
telephone
telegraph
television
telescope

trans *(across)*
transform
transgress
transmit
transaction

tri *(three)*
triangular
trimester
trioxide
trilogy

ultra *(above)*
ultramarine
ultramodern
ultraviolet
ultraconservative

un *(not)*
unbalanced
unawares
unabridged
undiscriminating

uni *(one)*
unification
unicycle
uniform
unilaterally

under *(below)*
undercharge
undercover
undergraduate
underground

F. Roots

act (*do*)
active
enactment
inactivity
reaction

aer (*of air*)
aerodynamic
aerobics
aerate
aerial

ast (*star*)
astronomy
asterisk
astrophysics
aster

bio (*life*)
biography
biologist
biomedical
biotechnology

cept (*take*)
interception
deceptive
receptivity
precept

cess (*move*)
procession
concessionary
abscess
cessation

cord (*heart*)
accord
discord
recording
cordial

cracy (*government*)
democracy
autocracy
aristocracy
theocracy

cure (*care*)
security
curator
insecure
curative

cycl (*circle*)
bicycle
cyclical
cyclist
cyclone

dic (*say*)
dictating
edict
dictator
prediction

duct (*lead*)
abduct
conductor
production
aqueduct

fact (*make*)
factor
manufactured
satisfaction
factory

fil (*line*)
profile
defilement
filament
misfiling

found (*bottom*)
foundation
founder
profoundly
confounded

fuse (*pour out*)
confusing
profusion
infuse
refusal

geo (*earth*)
geography
geocentric
geologist
geometrical

gram (*write*)
grammatical
ideogram
gramophone
telegram

graph (*write*)
photograph
graphically
autobiography
telegraph

gress (*go*)
progression
congressional
regressive
digress

meter (*measure*)
kilometer
thermometer
geometrical
metronome

miss (*send*)
transmission
submissive
missile
missionary

muse (*ponder*)
amusement
music
museum
bemused

pass (*suffer*)
compassion
passionate
passivity
impassioned

path (*feeling*)
pathology
sympathetic
telepathy
pathos

pend (*hang*)
independent
appendix
suspended
impending

phono (*sound*)
telephone
phonograph
phonetics
gramophone

photo (*light*)
photographer
photosynthesis
photocopy
unphotogenic

ply (fill)
reply
appliance
complying
imply

port (*carry*)
transport
portable
report
deported

pose (*put*)
depose
imposition
composer
exposed

prove (*test*)
improvement
proved
approval
reprove

psych (*mind*)
psychological
psychotherapy
psychopathic
psychic

quest (*seek*)
requested
inquest
questioning
conquest

sane (*health*)
insane
sanitary
sanitation
sanity

script (*write*)
postscript
inscription
conscripted
scriptural

sect (*cut*)
dissect
sector
intersection
sect

serve (*keep*)
conservation
preserves
reserving
servitude

sign (*mark*)
signature
designer
consignment
significance

sist (*stand*)
persistence
subsist
resisting
assisted

spec (*look*)
spectator
introspection
inspect
spectacles

stance (*stand*)
instance
circumstance
constancy
substantial

tact (*touch*)
tactile
tactless
contacted
intact

techn (*science*)
technology
technique
technical
pyrotechnology

test (*witness*)
attest
protesting
contestant
testimony

therm (*heat*)
thermometer
thermal
thermostat
hypothermia

tour (*turn*)
detour
tourism
entourage
contours

tract (*draw*)
retraction
attractive
protractor
tractable

verb (*word*)
verbally
proverb
reverberate
verbose

vers (*turn*)
reversal
introversion
conversions
subversive

vis (*see*)
envisage
invisible
visibility
visual

voc (*call*)
vocational
vocal
invocation
vocabulary

G. Suffixes

able *(capable)*
allowable
agreeable
unforgettable
negotiable

ance *(state)*
tolerance
endurance
vigilance
elegance

ar *(like)*
muscular
glandular
particular
irregular

ary *(connection)*
revolutionary
momentary
temporary
dictionary

ate *(cause)*
validate
liberate
exaggerate
encapsulate

en *(becoming)*
enlighten
forgotten
unwritten
lengthen

ence *(state)*
inference
preference
existence
obedience

ent *(quality)*
solvent
incompetent
magnificent
benevolent

ful *(full)*
insightful
reproachful
mirthful
prayerful

hood *(condition)*
fatherhood
likelihood
childhood
womanhood

ial *(pertaining to)*
essential
presidential
influential
circumstantial

ism *(practice)*
mechanism
realism
heroism
nationalism

ion *(state)*
description
verification
celebration
satisfaction

ist *(person)*
journalist
biologist
humorist
ophthalmologist

ity *(quality)*
rarity
humidity
antigravity
clarity

ive *(tendency)*
subjective
selective
unobtrusive
deceptive

ize *(cause)*
idealize
neutralize
serialize
familiarize

less *(less)*
voiceless
weightless
harmless
defenseless

ment *(state of)*
management
arrangement
parliament
establishment

ness *(quality)*
goodness
effectiveness
wickedness
jauntiness

or *(person who)*
counselor
auditor
contributor
predecessor

ous *(full of)*
glamorous
continuous
meticulous
mysterious

ship *(art)*
friendship
penmanship
horsemanship
workmanship

NOTES

Use these pages to keep a record of the strategies that work best for you.

NOTES